Life Is Hard but God Is Good

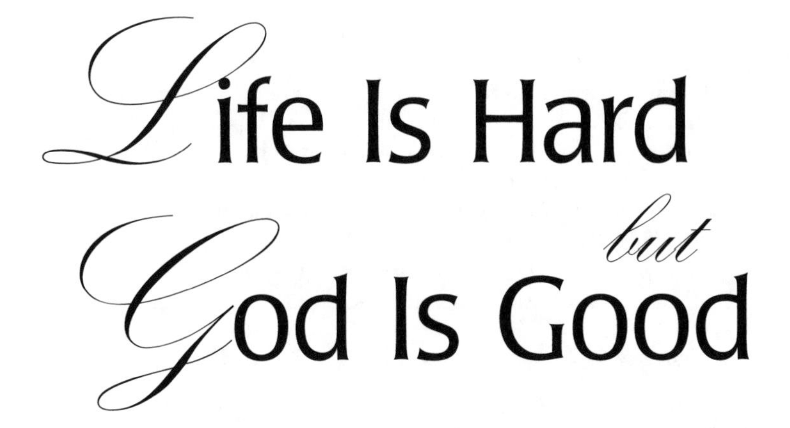

Life Is Hard but God Is Good

An Inquiry into Suffering

Adele J. Gonzalez

Maryknoll, New York 10545

Founded in 1970, Orbis Books endeavors to publish works that enlighten the mind, nourish the spirit, and challenge the conscience. The publishing arm of the Maryknoll Fathers & Brothers, Orbis seeks to explore the global dimensions of the Christian faith and mission, to invite dialogue with diverse cultures and religious traditions, and to serve the cause of reconciliation and peace. The books published reflect the views of their authors and do not represent the official position of the Maryknoll Society. To learn more about Maryknoll and Orbis Books, please visit our website at www.maryknollsociety.org.

Published by Orbis Books, Maryknoll, NY 10545-0302.

Manufactured in the United States of America.

Library of Congress Cataloging-in-Publication Data

Gonzalez, Adele J.
Life is hard but God is good : an inquiry into suffering / Adele J. Gonzalez.
p. cm.
Includes bibliographical references.
ISBN 978-1-57075-926-0 (pbk.)
1. Consolation. 2. Suffering—Religious aspects—Catholic Church. I. Title.

BX2373.S5G66 2011
248.8'6—dc22

2010050678

Contents

Introduction 1

1 The Journey to Understanding Begins 5

2 Seeking and Finding God 19

3 The Mystery of Evil 57

4 Understanding Anger and Forgiveness 99

5 The Mystery of Suffering 115

6 Understanding Faith 150

Epilogue 176

Notes 179

Introduction

A few years ago, I was the keynote speaker at a ministry conference. My lecture was on spirituality, and I was emphasizing the unconditional love of God. In the middle of the speech a gentleman raised his hand. I was surprised but invited him to speak. "How do you explain so much suffering in the world?" he asked. "How can a good God allow so many catastrophes that destroy people's lives each day?"

Everyone in the room became involved in the discussion. What began as a lecture became a dialogue with a lively assembly.

But my luck ran out when one gentleman objected: "This discussion is very interesting, but I came here looking for answers by the experts, by those who have devoted their lives to the study of theology. You are the speaker, and you came from far away, so please, what is your answer to the question of suffering? If God is good, why is life so hard?"

One could hear a pin drop in the room. They expected me to have an answer; otherwise, why had I been invited to give the speech?

I instantly looked at all the answers in my memory disk and the different angles from which we could look at the mystery of evil and suffering. I could have talked about the consequences of individual and social sin, original sin, or the mystery of evil, but I didn't go there. I will never know what possessed me at that moment, but on that sunny, warm morning in the land of the sun, I simply said, "Shit happens!" to more than three hundred people attending a ministry conference. I could not believe what I had said to such a professional gathering. But suddenly, everyone started to clap and laugh. I was not ready for that—and even less for what followed.

A Catholic bishop stood up in front of the audience and said, "This is the most profound explanation of evil I have ever heard!"

More than six years have passed since that conference, and I have not forgotten the insights that followed from my inappropriate words. It was a great conversation starter. I have continued to ponder the many questions asked that day and, above all, the multiple answers that were offered. Today, more than ever, I continue to hear the questions, Why does God allow or cause so much suffering? Isn't God all goodness?

Wars, terrorism, unemployment, crimes, illness and disease, natural disasters, scandals in church and government, fears and insecurities. Where is God in all this?

Many people find it impossible to believe in God—and even less in a "good" God—in the face of such suffering in the world. Unable to face a painful faith journey filled with unanswerable questions, they join the ranks of those who call our times "the age of despair." Many lose themselves in the cheap tabloids and loud talk shows with their messages of blame and doom. In a frantic search for security and clear answers, many accept the predictions that the "mother of all wars" will happen in our lifetimes and that the four horsemen of the Apocalypse are heralding Armageddon. This situation may appear far out to others, but it actually reflects the terror and the confusion of the average person today. What the tabloids and cable talk shows are doing is another form of domestic terrorism, and we are giving in to it.

Is it enough to say, "shit happens," when looking at a world gone mad? Of course not. It is a two-word encapsulation of the state of the world that asks us to go deeply with honesty and sincerity and study what all of this means simply to get through our days with some sense of understanding and peace. As someone who tries to be a spiritual companion to others, that morning six years ago motivated me to dive into the questions if not come to some authentic answers. Everyone wants to know, if God is good, why is life so hard? Is there an answer at all?

It is to you, my fellow sojourner, that I dedicate this book, hoping that through real-life stories and theological musings, you will begin to encounter the God of goodness and compassion in the midst of your suffering and troubles. Together let us discover the energy of love that transcends the world. As a man of peace said in a world as mad as ours two thousand years ago, "I have told you these things, so that in me you may have peace. In this world you will have trouble. But take heart! I have overcome the world" (John 16:33 New International Version).

Chapter 1

The Journey to Understanding Begins

When I look at your heavens, the work of your fingers,
the moon and the stars that you have established;
what are human beings that you are mindful of them,
mortals that you care for them?

—Psalm 8:3-4

Even if I wanted to, it is impossible for me to ignore the question of God and suffering. Living and ministering in South Florida I have dealt with hurricanes, floods, immigrant issues, racism, violence, and many other evils. Every day I have to rekindle my own hope and my belief in the goodness of God. I often wonder if I am simply too optimistic by nature or if there is a real foundation for this hope of mine?

I have struggled with physical and emotional pain all my life. As a child I had terrible pain in my legs and back because of undiagnosed rheumatoid arthritis. Pain has been an unwelcome companion in my journey of faith.

Bedtime was the worst time of the day because the pain kept me awake most of the night. My grandmother used to sit by my bed and gently rub my legs with ointment while she repeated the words "*consumatún, consumatún, consumatún*" over and over. I had no idea what she was saying, but she knew a lot of "prayers" from Spain, and I figured this was one of them. Her prayer, her massages, and most of all her love got me through many difficult nights.

Last week when my brother and I were remembering those times, we suddenly realized, after all these years, that what Grandma was actually saying was *consumatum est* ("it is finished"), meaning my pain was finished, over, gone. We both laughed when we finally understood the meaning of her words. Interestingly, I remember the awful pain, but I do not remember suffering, because I had my loving grandmother massaging my legs and repeating the "magic" Latin words! I know now that the magic was her love and assurance.

I have also experienced prejudice and discrimination in ways that range from the sublime to the ridiculous. If I were to write the stories of my early years in the United States, one book would not be enough to contain them!

When I came from Cuba in 1962, I was sixteen years old, and did not speak any English. Yet there were some girls from wealthy backgrounds who had come to the United States to study prior to the Communist Revolution of 1959. As I struggled to complete my senior year in a Catholic high school, there was a sharp contrast between the behavior of that Cuban group and the American girls, who were clueless about this influx of foreign students into their school.

My Cuban "sisters" appeared embarrassed by this new group of young Cubans who did not speak English and were attending their school thanks to a scholarship from the Catholic Church. Those days were difficult, but the saddest part for me was that I got more help from the Americans who did not understand me than from the Cubans who were bilingual and in a position to be of assistance.

What was I to make of this situation? I remember not even knowing what subject matter was being taught until I saw the other girls open their books. I somehow conquered American history by memorizing most of the pages. If one of the essay questions included the name of George Washington, I would write several paragraphs that included everything that I remembered about him and his time. Needless to say, I had no idea about the content of my answers! I felt like a fake and an outsider. Nevertheless, I made it, and in a year I graduated from high school.

Something very different happened when I started college. By then I knew some English, but I also knew that I was an alien. I had not been born with that condition; I became one after leaving my country as a teenager to live in exile.

I was unquestionably different from the other young women. This became painfully real when, during my freshman year, my roommate asked if it had been hard for me to get used to wearing clothes. When I tried to understand what she meant, she said, "Don't you all wear simple coverups similar to Tarzan and Jane on your island?"

Obviously this was 1962, and the Cuban culture and way of life were not well known in South Florida especially to people from the Midwest. Yet I was speechless. No offense had been intended, no desire to hurt me, but I still remember my feelings of alienation and strangeness, of being in a place other than home. The exchange was caused by ignorance, but it resulted in hurt. Ignorance has the power to hurt and destroy not only individuals, but entire communities, even nations.

Should I have considered both my high school and college experiences sufferings allowed by a good God to teach me something or to make me stronger? Were they examples of ignorance and lack of information or simply another moment in which "shit happened"? These were big questions, and I had no answers for any of them. After thinking about them for a long time, I humbly acknowledged that unquestionably shit happens!

In what is now my home, the United States, we saw evil face to face in the terrorist attacks of September 11, 2001. For the first time, we Americans experienced on our own soil the terror, despair, and powerlessness that other nations live with each day. How could those impressive and powerful towers be destroyed in broad daylight as people watched in disbelief and the television cameras rolled as if filming a horror movie?

The good God that blesses America from the mountains to the prairies could not have caused that destruction. Someone else was responsible, and soon a group claimed responsibility for the attack: Islamic fundamentalist terrorists. Once we knew the perpetrators, we quickly demonized all Muslims. They were "evil," and we had to eradicate this evil from the face of the earth. Somehow, this crusade translated into the invasion of Iraq, and once again we solved a very complicated question in a simplistic and ignorant manner: war!

Four years later, America suffered another catastrophe, hurricane Katrina, which devastated New Orleans. The city's levees were not built to hold the power of a massive hurricane and collapsed under its destructive winds and waters. The entire world saw firsthand the poverty and misery of the black community in that city. Many Americans were shocked. How could there be so many poor families in the greatest nation on earth? We all witnessed the "evil" that Katrina unveiled: city leaders blamed state leaders who in turn blamed the federal government. This monstrous storm will remain in our history books as the ultimate example of public embarrassment in the land of the free and opportunity for all.

Did God send Katrina to expose racism and poverty, or maybe to punish us? Some affirmed that New Orleans deserved this evil because of its loose lifestyle and unorthodox religious practices. Some people felt good blaming the city for its own drama, thus letting God off the hook. The face of suffering that appeared each day on our television sets was being dismissed by some, because, after all, "they did it to themselves."

Of course, FEMA (Federal Emergency Management Agency) and the other government agencies did not respond fast enough and, for many, that explained the drama without having to assign any role to God. As time passed and the reconstruction process began, I read that the New Orleans School Board identified Katrina as the best thing that ever happened to their educational system. Because of the public exposure, the city would now have better schools and the necessary books and teaching materials that had been previously lacking.

Blessing, a hurricane? I don't think so.

A few years later, I watched horrified the cruel and meaningless loss of lives and the total destruction caused by the earthquake in Haiti. The old question echoed again in my heart: Why did God let this atrocity happen? This catastrophe touched me personally. I have many Haitian friends, and over half of the members of my parish are Haitians. How do I explain to them the suffering and the chaos caused by this earthquake?

A very good friend of mine wrote this e-mail:

> We have been looking for one of my nieces who lost her husband. I just got the news that she spent three days in front of the building where her husband died until they pulled him out and they held the funeral in front of the rubble yesterday. She never left the place until then. Thank you for your prayers and support.

The following day I saw my friend and learned that the previous information was inaccurate. Two weeks after the earthquake, her niece was still sitting in front of the rubble waiting for the body of her husband to be recovered and buried. Where was God in all this?

Haitians are a spiritual and religious people; 80 percent of the population is Catholic. To them God *is*, and God is good. *La vie est dure, mais Dieu est bon* (Life is hard, but God is good), which implies that life and God are not the same. With such strong faith, why had God forsaken them? This question is heard not only among ordinary people, but even in news reports. Some answers were so sick that I wondered which was the greater evil, the earthquake or the manner in which some religious fundamentalists explained the event.

To say that the earthquake was the consequence of a voodoo deal made by some Haitians and Satan many years ago is preposterous. It is sad that even spiritual leaders have such a narrow and limited image of God. When a previous earthquake hit Mexico City some years earlier, various televangelists similarly explained that the disaster was God's punishment of the Mexican people for their heretical worship of Our Lady of Guadalupe.

How can anyone who believes in the God revealed by Jesus the Christ think that way? What kind of God are we presenting to the world? No wonder the English writer G. K. Chesterton affirmed, "The Christian ideal has not been tried and found wanting; it has been found difficult and left untried."[1] The God of Jesus the Christ has remained hidden from the world because of the ignorance and indifference of many Christians. We have failed to reveal to our struggling world the compassionate face of our loving God.

Where is the evil in these situations? Could its roots be in flawed and prejudiced human actions and not in God? Could it be that the destruction in New Orleans and Port-au-Prince was caused by poor building codes, nonexistent substructures, and years of ignoring the unsustainable conditions of the two cities—what we call "social sin"? Can we blame it on God and God's way of punishing people? Or is it simply that bad things happen, and God is found in our response to them?

As I write these pages, the fight to contain the oil and gas spewing into the Gulf of Mexico goes on; thousands of barrels poured into the Gulf a mile below the surface. I cannot even begin to fathom the consequences of this tragic incident. The waters are totally contaminated, animals are dying, the marsh in the Louisiana coast is being destroyed, and fishers, shrimpers, and hotels have lost their means of income.

It is impossible to watch the raping of creation and the destruction of small, honest, centuries-old small businesses without questioning the goodness of God. I am using strong words, because they reflect my feelings every time I watch or hear the news. Most people put all the responsibility on British Petroleum (BP), but is that the end of the story? Are the rest of us innocent bystanders? One more time disaster strikes close to home, and we wonder if maybe God should also share the blame with BP and the government. People ask, as they always have: How can a good God allow good people to suffer like that?

The question of God and suffering shapes the way we relate to God and affects our capacity to hope in the presence of evil. Many writers have expressed that what the world needs today is hope, and I agree. This lack of hope is partially caused by a thwarted understanding of God and creation, as well as a limited personal relationship with the God who *is* love (see 1 John 4:16). This I learned the hard way from my own story.

One way of dealing with any "mystery" is through stories; after all, when Jesus tried to explain the mystery of the reign of God to his friends, he used parables, stories—"The reign of God is like. . . ." Stories such as these have always helped me to reflect on the mysteries of God, goodness, and evil in my own life.

My First Encounter with God

There is one story that includes God, evil, and suffering, and it was perhaps the most painful experience of my life. It happened when I did not know God, and I am sure that without this dramatic event I would never have encountered the God of love, goodness, and compassion that I know today.

My father died suddenly a few days before my fourteenth birthday. It was an unquestionable evil. He was a Mason, and although my mother had been raised a Catholic, they were not married in the Church. My mother worked out her guilt by taking my brother and me to Mass every Sunday while my father waited outside in the car. How I hated those Sundays! I found the Latin Mass boring, the sermons out of touch with my reality, and the rituals meaningless. Deep in my heart I had sided with my father's anticlericalism and mistrust of religion.

The custom in Cuba, as in many European countries, was to go home for lunch every day. My brother, being the youngest, had a different schedule and rode the school bus. I only had afternoon sessions, and every day after lunch my father would drop me off at school, then take my mother to her office, and finally go to his own office.

On this particular day, he left me at school as usual and then took my mother to work. Something unexpected happened when he got to his office. As was his custom, he took the elevator, and when the doors opened on his floor he collapsed of a massive heart attack and died instantaneously. I learned about these details later.

All I remember was being called to the principal's office, where our aunt and uncle were waiting for my brother and me because "Papá had taken very ill." We rode a taxi home. It did not take too long for me to ask my aunt, "He is not sick, he is dead, right?" With that simple question the drama began and our family was turned upside down. Mother felt apart, and so did our lives.

That evening at the funeral home, I remember touching my father's cold body in the casket and, with a broken heart, asking, "Where is my father?" This is not the gentle, intelligent, and loving man who helped me each night with my math homework! This is an empty shell! I did not have an answer then, and I lived with that question for over a year while everyone around me was blaming God or the doctors for the tragedy.

One day a classmate who belonged to a Catholic youth group invited me to a retreat. I had no idea what a retreat was, but I went with her and quickly found my "answers": there was a heaven and a hell—of course my father was in the latter. In addition, I was an illegitimate child because my parent's marriage had not been blessed by the Catholic Church. If I ever wanted to become a sister, the priest directing the retreat solemnly said, I could not because of my illegitimacy.

The last day of the weekend retreat I went to confession. I entered the dark box, knelt, and through the screen told this stranger that my father was in hell and that I was responsible for it. What followed was the first of many miracles. Ignoring my "mortal sin" and without giving me absolution, the priest (a different priest from the one directing the retreat) asked me if I would wait until the others had received the sacrament and then go back and introduce myself. He said, "This is a very interesting conversation and I would like to continue it later outside the box and with more time." Of course, as a teenager I was flattered by the attention and agreed to meet him later.

When confessions ended, I approached the priest and identified myself as the person who had sent her father to hell. He invited me to his office, where I confessed that I was not a good Catholic and that if I had been more committed and devoted, I could have converted my father because of his love for me. My lack of faith had precipitated his perdition!

The good man took in my words without saying anything, and after a few minutes of introductions and chit-chat, he asked me what kind of a person my father had been. For a long time I described this loving, gentle man who had migrated from Spain at age sixteen and had always put the needs of others before his. He adored my mother and was the best possible father to my brother and me. My father had many friends who looked up to him because of his goodness, generosity, honesty, and sense of humor. In addition, my father loved the music from his native Spain and the classics, something we both shared. He was a man of peace, at peace with himself and with the One he called "the Creator of this wonderful universe."

When I finished, the priest asked me to close my eyes and imagine that I was God standing at the entrance to heaven. He used my vivid imagination to ask if I could see my father walking in the distance wondering where to go. Obviously, this experience lasted longer than this story, but after a few minutes, he said, "What would you do?" Without hesitating for even a second I responded, "I would run to him, give him a big hug and a kiss and bring him with me into my heaven!"

After a long pause to savor the moment, the priest surprised me with another question: "What makes you think that you are more compassionate and loving than God?" Totally embarrassed I said, "I did not mean that! Of course I am not better than God." With a smile I will never forget, he said, "Do you know God?" I replied, "No." He continued, "Would you like to know God?" I quickly said, "Yes!" He then invited me to come to his office every week with all the questions I had about God, faith, religion, or anything else. He said, "The sky is the limit, and there are no wrong or stupid questions."

> *So he set off and went to his father. But while he was still far off, his father saw him and was filled with compassion; he ran and put his arms around him and kissed him.*
>
> —Luke 15:20

During my remaining time in Cuba (about two years), I faithfully met with the priest once a week. On that first encounter, this holy man had taught me the parable of the Prodigal Son without using a Bible or any other book. It was not until later that I realized that I had given to my father the same embrace that the father in the parable had given to his youngest son. A miracle in the midst of all the apparent evil: Catholic priests did not usually pay this kind of attention to a contrite teenager in 1961!

My father's passing was probably the most difficult time in my life. Yet because of it I came to know the God who has sustained me until now, the God capable of creating a wonderful universe where Catholics and Masons coexist.

The image of God presented in chapter 15 of the Gospel of Luke was my father's gift to me, "the Pharisees and the scribes were grumbling and saying, 'This fellow [Jesus] welcomes sinners and eats with them'" (15:2). I do not think I am off base when I connect my experience to the following Scripture passages:

> *I will not leave you orphaned; I am coming to you.*
>
> —John 14:18

> *I tell you the truth: it is to your advantage that I go away, for if I do not go away, the Advocate will not come to you.*
>
> —John 16:7

I never felt abandoned by my father, because his leaving brought into my life a deep awareness of God in whom my father also lived. The conversation with the priest showed me that if I, a simple human being, was capable of such love and compassion for my father, how much more the Creator God would love him. He was after all the beloved Son of God.

Over forty-five years have gone by, and I still consider that moment my first and deepest encounter with the God who is love. Every time I think about it, my spirit recalls the praises of God sung by Francis of Assisi:

> You are holy, Lord, the only God,
> and your deeds are wonderful . . .
> You are good, all good, supreme good . . .
> You are love. You are wisdom.

You are humility. You are endurance.
You are rest. You are peace.
You are joy and gladness . . .
You suffice for us.

Did God take my father at an early age and leave us alone so that I would have faith? I could not possibly believe in such a God! What then? How do I explain this evil turned into a blessing in my life?

I have learned through this and many other personal experiences that we can recognize something as good only if we have known something else as bad. How can we say that we feel well, if we have never been sick? How can we recognize the forgiveness and compassion of God if we do not know about punishment and retribution? How can we appreciate light, if we have never experienced darkness? Why would we desire a glass of fresh water if we did not know what thirst is?

In my life, good and evil seem to go hand in hand, the two sides of the same coin. Do I dare say that one cannot exist without the other? I could not have appreciated the God who is always present without the experience of my father's absence.

Yet the questions remain: Who is God? What is evil? Why suffer? As I said before, to me the root of the problem is a narrow and misconstrued image of God. Thus I start with my search and experience of God, the purported cause of all evil and the scapegoat of all "innocent bystanders."

Chapter 2

Seeking and Finding God

Moses said to God, "If I come to the Israelites and say to them, 'The God of your ancestors has sent me to you,' and they ask me, 'What is his name?' what shall I say to them?" God said to Moses, "I AM WHO I AM."
—Exodus 3:13-14

This passage from Exodus contains a puzzling answer. This is not the kind of name that Moses expected to hear (a verb more than a noun), but at the same time it was the perfect answer: "I am." It seems that God is taunting Moses, "What more can I say? How else could I explain my being in a way that you could understand?"

To me, the answer is elusive yet all-encompassing: I AM! It stems from the Hebrew monotheistic belief that God, the uncreated Creator, does not depend on anything or anyone to *be*. Many religious traditions have attempted to define the term, but ultimately, "this divine name is mysterious just as God is mystery. It is at once a name revealed and something like the refusal of a name, and hence it better expresses God as what he is—infinitely above everything that we can understand or say."[1]

Through the experience of my father's death and in the years that followed, I continued to deepen my understanding of God. But slowly I became aware that to me God could not be anything other than *love*. The First Letter of John states, "God is love" (1 John 4:16). This statement rang true and was congruent with my experience. Yes, "God is love" and I was beginning to see as in a mirror this tremendous reality.

The God of Jesus the Christ

I was aware that, for Christians, God is the eternal being that created and preserves the universe, the uncaused cause, the unmoved mover. On the other hand, I also envisioned God in anthropomorphic terms; God speaks, hears, listens, and intervenes in human history as a benevolent parent committed to caring for her children. That image of God was certainly congruent with the God who welcomed my father into heaven. God was all powerful, all knowing, and at the same time, forgiving, loving, and compassionate. How could I reconcile these two attributes in the God I believed in?

My faith journey led me to the Hebrew and Christian Scriptures. I became fascinated with Jesus and the Gospel message. The attraction was not so much to Jesus as the Savior Messiah as to Jesus the giver of a new way of life, a man with a vision and knowledge of what the world was meant to be. Jesus challenged the people of his time to see beyond what their senses revealed and pointed to a new creation: the "reign of God" characterized by love, justice, and peace for all.

John the Baptist heard stories about this man healing diseases and preaching a new way, so he sent two of his disciples to ask Jesus, "'Are you the one who is to come, or are we to wait for another?' Jesus had just then cured many people of diseases, plagues, and evil spirits, and had given sight to many who were blind. And he answered them, 'Go and tell John what you have seen and heard: the blind receive their sight, the lame walk, the lepers are cleansed, the deaf hear, the dead are raised, and the poor have good news brought to them'" (Luke 7:20-22).

The message was clear, and the call to serve was implicit: if I wanted to be the woman that God created me to be, I had to bring good news to the poor, to heal lepers, to set the captives free, and to give sight to the blind.

I tried to begin at home. My mother was blind. She began to lose her vision as a result of glaucoma during the first years of the Cuban Revolution when there were no medicines available. By the time she came to the United States, she was totally blind. I have always been a lover of nature, and it pained me that she could not see the awesomeness of God's creation that I enjoyed so much.

Naturally, I could not restore my mother's sight, but she helped me understand that her blindness was of no consequence compared to the blindness of most of the "seeing" people she knew. As years passed I realized that spiritual blindness, thirst, and hunger were worse than all the physical problems I was trying to solve. People were spiritually starved and dehydrated, but did not know it.

After reading, studying and praying the Gospels, I knew that

- *I was meant to help the spiritually blind who were unable to see God in their lives. I wanted to enable them to see with the eyes of faith.* Every day I meet people who cannot identify God's presence and activity in their lives. Because I am a professional lay minister, some assume that I must be "closer to God." I feel very uncomfortable when they ask me, "Would you speak to God on my behalf?" They do not trust the love of God who is available to anyone, no favoritism!
- *I was called to help those paralyzed by fear to walk in trust.* Because of my experience with physical and emotional pain and the conviction that God is with me every step of the way, I have the credibility to help others to trust. I have been almost "paralyzed" by fear many times, and my own story gives others the strength to take the leap of faith and trust in God's providence.
- *The HIV/AIDS victims, the homeless, the immigrants, the impure of our world today needed to be cleansed.* As an alien, I understand the alienation of others in this group. They see in me an equal, someone who understands their feelings. Because of my own need for healing, I can be a presence to them in their own healing process.
- *I desired with all my heart to help those who could not "hear" the voice of God because of fear or past hurts.* I often share the stories of my father's death, my mother's blindness, and other difficult times in my life. I explain that for a long time my own anger or desolation prevented me from hearing the voice of God. As I look back with the eyes of faith I know that God was present with me in the situation.

- *The dead, the sleeping, the lethargic Christians sitting in our churches on Sunday needed to be brought back to life*. A priest friend of mine once told me how hard it was for him to celebrate Mass with a congregation of "unconverted" people. He said, "I have given up the hope of getting some energy from them in my low days. They read the bulletin and never look at the altar where the Banquet is being celebrated."
- *And the poor deserved to hear the good news of God's love for them, of "my" love for them, and of society's concern for them*. It has been said that the worth of a society is measured by the way it treats its poorest members. Our culture has failed the test, and I also have failed many times. I know that the love, peace, and justice of the reign of God have to become a reality in our poorest neighborhoods.

These were the radical consequences of my belief in the God revealed by Jesus the Christ in my life journey. I had come to know God, I had heard the Gospel call, and now I had to respond.

Jesus spoke about his Father as the one who "makes his sun rise on the evil and on the good, and sends rain on the righteous and on the unrighteous" (Matthew 5:45). Jesus also asked his followers to love their enemies, to do good and lend expecting nothing in return, so that in so doing, they would become "children of the Most High; for he is kind to the ungrateful and the wicked" (Luke 6:35). I was definitely attracted to the *Abba* of Jesus; it was the same God I had met many years before when my father died!

The more I found God through and in Jesus, the more I felt called to serve. Love and service seemed to be the core values of Jesus of Nazareth. I wanted to serve as Jesus served! This strong calling led me to professional lay ecclesial ministry in the Catholic Church. It was during this period that I began keeping a spiritual journal. The following entry describes the image of God that was emerging better than I could today:

Journal
September 22, 1972
2:00 P.M.
"Jesus, the revelation of a broken God"

Yahweh can only become my God through the revelation of Jesus the Christ. Jesus is the Word of God! Jesus is the epiphany of God!

He brings to me a "strange" new image of God:

Failure
Suffering
Pain
Death
Misunderstanding
Humiliation
Brokenness

All these experiences are accepted as an integral part of the human person, but they are foreign to our concept of the divine, of God.

Jesus came to tell us that in his humanity, he is revealing God.

"Philip said to him, 'Lord, show us the Father, and we will be satisfied.' Jesus said to him, 'Have I been with you all this time, Philip, and you still do not know me? Whoever has seen me has seen the Father'" (John 14:8-9).

If this Jesus is the total revelation of God, I want to look at him more carefully. . . . I want to take more time to get to know this man who is showing me a revolutionary concept of God.

"After he had washed their feet . . . he said to them, 'Do you know what I have done to you?'" (John 13:12).

This man serves. This man is giving himself for his friends. But he still needs to ask, "Do you know? Do you understand?"

"Lord, if you had been here, my brother would not have died" (John 11:32).

(*My version*) Jesus, I don't care if you are sad because your best friend is dead. You should have been here . . . available . . . always present. Who told you that you were allowed to take breaks? You are my "problem solver." Where were you when I needed you? I want you here with me always. I demand your presence—after all, you are God.

I am sick, I feel very limited and I want you to be like my grandmother, always by my side!

"*I am thirsty.*" God is thirsty!

"*My God, my God, why have you forsaken me*?"

"My people, my people, I am a forsaken God!"

"Now is my soul troubled. And what shall I say?"

God's soul is troubled.

Jesus refuses to be a man like any other of his time. Many before tried to walk the same path and eventually gave up, or people realized they were charlatans.

Unless you are totally one with God, you cannot help humanity become divine.

If you had given up, I would have never known the depth, the width, and the height of God's love. This love goes beyond welcoming my Father with open arms. After all, my father was a great man, but you, Jesus, promised paradise to a criminal hanging on a cross next to you. My mind cannot fully grasp this craziness!

I must admit that many times you upset my logical mind . . .

Did you think that I, your Creator, would be sitting on a comfortable throne in heaven watching you suffer? I tried to make myself known to you, but you failed to recognize me in Nazareth, in Jerusalem, in Gethsemane, on Golgotha. . . .

Yes, I am a broken God, and I refuse to be any other way!

Even now, "as you do to one of the least of my brothers or sisters, you do it to me." I choose to stay and be broken over and over again.

How sad, but I wouldn't have it any other way. My nature is to give life, to love, to create, to always become more and more who I am.

And I am life, love, compassion, forgiveness, justice, goodness. . . . Yes, these are feelings! I am a God who feels and loves passionately. I am the Living God!

I am in the air that you breathe;
I am in the wind that you ride;
I am in the song that you sing;
I am in the tears that you cry.
I am living water;
I am dance and song;
I am pain and sorrow;
I am fire and love.
I am the one living God;
I am the fountain of life;
I have come to bring you peace;
You are unique and you are mine.

For many years this God sustained me. I was happy proclaiming the good news of Jesus the Christ, the love of God, and God's compassion and forgiveness. Standing on the social teachings of the Church, I gave assistance to the poor and was an advocate for their needs.

I worked among farm workers and defended their cause; I also served as chaplain on the mental health floor of a community hospital. The institutional Church provided the structures that allowed me to serve. I felt united to Jesus and his mission. My ministry was rewarding, I was following in his footsteps!

God of the Universe

After many years of archdiocesan and parish ministry, I began to realize how narrow my vision of God was now becoming. While repeating rituals, celebrating sacraments, and teaching "official" Catholic beliefs, I had put Jesus in a neat package wrapped with multicolored ribbons. I had made him very attractive but also small enough to fit my "image and likeness."

In order to serve as pastoral minister, I always had the needs of the people before my eyes. "What do they really need?" was my constant question. I found out that what they really needed was an intimate relationship with Jesus. We cannot deny how attractive the historical Jesus is for Christians. The stories of his life, the teachings and miracles, his passion, death, and resurrection have kept audiences spellbound for centuries. The Shroud of Turin is a good example of the fascination with his humanity, his possible looks, height, the color of his eyes, and so on.

Moreover, the emphasis of Catholic doctrine on the role of Jesus as Savior limited his mission to that of the "Lamb of God" who came to take away the sin of the world. Everyone is familiar with the Servant Song in Isaiah 53:3-6:

He was despised and rejected by others
a man of suffering and acquainted with infirmity . . .
Surely he has borne our infirmities
and carried our diseases;
yet we accounted him stricken,
struck down by God, and afflicted.
But he was wounded for our transgressions,
crushed for our iniquities;
upon him was the punishment that made us whole,
and by his bruises we are healed.
All we like sheep have gone astray;
we have all turned to our own way,
and the LORD *has laid on him*
the iniquity of us all.

After a while I found myself talking and teaching about Jesus as the poor victim who had to die to pay for the sins of humanity before an angry God. This bothered me.

As my journal entry demonstrated before, the incarnation was central in my faith. Jesus was the revelation of the invisible God. Sadly, for most Christians, the emphasis was on redemption. It went back to original sin as a fundamental alienation from God, a separation so profound that only God could "fix it." Thus, Jesus, the Word made flesh, was God's action to right our original wrong. There was a good reason why this approach became the better known and widely accepted view.

In the New Testament we read how early Christians tried to find meaning to Jesus' suffering and violent death. They also needed an explanation for their own sufferings. They looked for answers in the Old Testament and in the Semitic mentality preserved in books written seven to eight hundred years before Christ. They found laments and complaints from righteous and just men who had suffered through no fault of their own: Job, the innocent victim; Abraham, sacrificing his son Isaac; and others. The suffering of the just seemed to fit the death of Jesus.

In the early Christian communities these stories colored the entire story of Jesus, including the meaning of his birth and life. This was especially true in the Gospels of Mark, Matthew, and Luke, who wrote for the persecuted Christians. The sufferings of their Messiah gave then hope and encouragement.

Throughout the centuries, Christian theology and piety continued and further developed these interpretations of Jesus' suffering and death, namely, as a means of atonement for our sins. The purpose of Jesus' life was linked to original sin and human sinfulness. Thus, without sin, there would have been no need for the incarnation. In this approach, God's love was demonstrated in his willingness to forgive us and offer us salvation after the fall.

I realized that using this language in teaching, praying, and liturgical celebrations did violence to me, spiritually and physically. The physical pain that was my faithful companion increased as a result of stress, and, above all, my spiritual body was getting sick and spiritually dehydrated.

New questions were emerging: Was Jesus the revelation of God only for Christians? Could I find God outside the institutional Church? Was the awesome Creator that I knew the sole possession of a few million people who attended church on Sundays? Was Jesus the Savior of just human beings? What would happen if there was life somewhere else in the universe? Would the incarnation have happened if we had not sinned?

I was feeling uncomfortable seeing Jesus as the brilliant idea that God came up with when we blew our chances in the Garden of Eden. The prayers that I read every day in the Roman Missal spoke only of this Lord and Savior who had died for my sins. In addition, Jesus' salvation worked only for a few who met strict qualifications as taught and interpreted by the various Christian denominations. I was maturing and developing as a person and as a professional, and my image of God began to change once again.

I had to find another way to understand Jesus and the God he came to reveal. My former center was not holding anymore! But God was present in my searching, although I did not know it.

Since my young adult years I had been fascinated by the writings of the Jesuit priest Pierre Teilhard de Chardin. His ideas captivated me, although I did not fully understand them. The God that emerged from his writings was a cosmic, awesome God who created by uniting in love. This God went beyond the historical Jesus, the miracles, the parables; this God transcended all the elements that were familiar to me and my still-mythical faith. I found my own discomfort expressed in Teilhard's words:

> Sometimes people think that they can increase your attraction in my eyes by stressing almost exclusively the charm and goodness of your human life in the past. But truly, O Lord, if I wanted to cherish only a man, then I would surely turn to those whom you have given me in the allurement of their present flowering. Are there not, with our mothers, brothers, friends and sisters, enough irresistibly lovable people around us? Why should we turn to Judaea

> two thousand years ago? No, what I cry out for, like every being, with my whole life and all my earthly passion, is something very different from an equal to cherish: it is a God to adore.[2]

These words clarified my own uneasiness. The Jesus I knew was a historical figure who in words and actions taught me a new way of being. But, as I grew in awareness of the vastness of the universe, I needed more. Teilhard helped me understand that I was searching for more than "an equal to cherish"; I was looking for a God to adore!

In an interview with the *National Catholic Reporter,* Franciscan friar Richard Rohr asked, "What about creation as a whole? How far back and forward in time does the Christ figure extend, and who exactly is Christ?"[3] I had very similar doubts. The historical Jesus could not be the center of the universe unfolding before my eyes.

My questions were taking new existential proportions. I felt that the gentle God who had welcomed my father into heaven was fading away, and a new image was slowly emerging. I wanted to hold on to my "old" God, but I also needed to be open to the new that I sensed approaching. These were difficult times spiritually.

Who was actually the God I believed in? How could he be a man-God who lived on this planet over two thousand years ago and at the same time the unchangeable, omnipotent, omniscient, and impassible (unable to feel) God of traditional theology?

I slowly and gently began to grow in a new consciousness of God. As I continue to write this chapter, I turn to one of my journals again:

Journal
October 5, 1980
11:00 A.M.
Hermitage in Maryland

I am stretched out in the sand. I was listening to the music of the ocean and enjoying the gentle kiss of the warm sun.

I thought: "God is touching me," and I laughed.

But it was more than that! It is more than that!

It's a sacred moment of union of the divine out-there with the divine within me.

It's the moment when the eternal Creator becomes one with all creatures in the Cosmic Christ. This moment of passionate love is called "Incarnation" by some; "Spirit" by others; "Cosmic Dance" by a few, and now "higher consciousness" by a growing number of people.

This is the moment of liberation for God. This is the moment when in time and space, God at last becomes what God is: self-giving love.

This is the moment when the face of God is changed by the waves and tsunamis of humanity.

The transcendent Creator God of the sun and the moon, of the ocean and the forest, could not kiss me if God were not also the suffering, liberated One already living in me.

It's my center touching the center of the universe, becoming one and celebrating the union for which I was created.

WOW!

The Trinitarian God

By this time, I was getting confused. I could not reconcile my friend Jesus who sat by my bed at night when I was in pain with this awesome God of the Big Bang dancing among the stars. I tried to look into the traditional Christian answer to this dilemma: the doctrine of the Trinity, One God, three persons. The Father was the Creator; the Son was the Savior who came to reveal the Father; and the Holy Spirit was the result of the love between the Father and the Son. But, for some reason, I found this explanation totally unappealing and irrelevant and of no help at all in my quest for the real God.

While teaching theology to undergraduate students at Barry University, I began to ask them, "Do you know what the doctrine of the Trinity means for Christians?"

Those who were not Christians had no clue, nothing, *nada!* A few of the Catholics or former Catholics proudly answered: "It means there are three persons in One God, the Father, the Son, and the Holy Ghost/Spirit."

One young man from Latin America told us that he knew the answer because his grandmother had explained it to him, and it was actually very simple. "It is like water, she had told him, "it can be in liquid form, or in gas, or frozen, but it always remains H_2O." The kid was so proud especially when the entire class clapped appreciating the wisdom of the grandmother. I was speechless!

The New Testament, which I love so much, was full of references to the Trinity: Father, Son, and Holy Spirit. I grew up making the Sign of the Cross and repeating the Triune formula. For years I had tried to respond to Jesus' call to, "Go . . . and make disciples of all nations, baptizing them in the name of the Father and of the Son and of the Holy Spirit" (Matthew 28:19). What was wrong with me? Why was I so turned off by this doctrine?

In my heart of hearts, I felt that the concept of the Holy Trinity portrayed a narcissistic God having fun and enjoying himself in an eternal dance with the Son and the Spirit. Every year on this feast I anticipated a homily about the wonderful inner life that the "three persons" enjoyed and how their love could serve as a model for the love that should exist in families. This parallel between God's internal life and a human family was totally absurd. I was so annoyed! What did this say about my loving, compassionate, and cosmic God? What did this wonderful inner life of the Trinity have to offer me, poor creature?

But the awesome God I believe in continued to work in strange ways! I was taking a graduate course on morality, and the topic came up. Some of my colleagues seemed to be into the trinitarian God while I listened in silence. Unexpectedly, the professor asked my opinion, and I honestly shared my thoughts. He told me that obviously I did not understand the trinitarian God, but he did not offer me any satisfactory explanation.

After class, one of the students asked me if I had read the book *God for Us* by Catherine Mowry La Cugna.[4] I had never heard of it, and she strongly recommended that I get it. She promised it would change my perception of the Trinity, and it did!

La Cugna explained the two traditional ways in which the doctrine has been approached:

1. *The theological approach*: the study of God's inner life, that is, the self-relatedness of Father, Son, and Spirit. This is the commonly known approach. Because of the emphasis and almost exclusive way of explaining the Trinity in this

manner, many (including me) have seen the Trinity as unrelated to us and intrinsically uninteresting. But the doctrine of the Trinity is not primarily a theory about God's inner life but an effort to articulate the basic faith of Christians.[5]

2. *The christological approach* (Economic Trinity): an entirely different way of approaching the doctrine, requiring that we root all our speculation about the triune nature of God in the self-communication of God in the person of Christ and in the activity of the Holy Spirit.[6] To talk about this approach, theologians use the term *oikonomia,* from *oikos* ("house") and *nomos* ("law"), therefore, "the law or administration of a household." In the Pauline tradition, the word *oikonomia* is used to describe *the providential plan of God for creation.* In time, this word became a synonym of the principal events that reveal the providence of God: the incarnation of Christ and the sending of the Holy Spirit.

Thus, when the doctrine of the Trinity is properly understood, it reveals the plan of God from the beginning: the affirmation of God's intimate communion with us through Jesus Christ in the Holy Spirit. The center of the trinitarian doctrine is the communion between God and us.

I found more insights about God's plan for creation in the Pauline tradition. Colossians 1:15-20 is one of the most important theological statements about the person of Christ in the New Testament. Christ is praised as the visible image of the God we cannot see; that is, he manifests God's presence in his person, and everything was created through him, in him, and for him. Therefore, he existed before all creation.

> *He is the image of the invisible God . . . in him all things in heaven and on earth were created, things visible and invisible, whether thrones or dominions or rulers or powers—all things have been created through him and for him. He himself is before all things, and in him all things hold together.*
>
> —Colossians 1:15-17

There is a well-known song entitled, "He's Got the Whole World in His Hands." Most Christians have heard it, but just a few get its meaning. The Word is holding the entire universe together; the Christ is the beginning and the end, the Alpha and the Omega (see Revelation 1:1-8).

This is not a chaotic creation waiting for cataclysms of apocalyptic proportions to destroy it. This universe follows an order, even when we do not understand it. There is a beginning, and that beginning is Christ, who is also the Omega Point, toward which everything is converging.

In the Gospel of John, Jesus is the personal manifestation of God in the world. In Jesus, the Word of God, for whom and in whom God created all things, became flesh (John 1:14). This Gospel is famous for Jesus' christological declarations of "I AM." They emphasize Jesus' divinity and are based on the name of God in the Hebrew Scriptures that I mentioned at the beginning of this chapter.

In spite of these biblical insights, there are pseudo-Christians who preach the destruction of the world, Armageddon, a battle between God and Satan. Taking the Book of Revelation literally and out of context, they predict cataclysms that will destroy all that is good in the universe. The sad part is that the goodness of the Creator and the fact that when "God saw everything that he had made . . . it was very good" (Genesis 1:31) get lost in this equation.

From the beginning of creation, God has tried to communicate and relate with all creatures. In the Judeo-Christian tradition, we believe that in ancient times God did so through events and the prophets. And in the fullness of time, God manifested God's oneness with humankind in Jesus Christ, and by the power of the Holy Spirit God continues to be present to us, seeking communion with all creatures.

My belief is that God became incarnate in Jesus of Nazareth because of a desire to be in relationship with creation, a desire that was there from the beginning. Looking at God from the perspective of the incarnation, of Jesus the Christ as the visible image of God, we find a God who is relational, who breaks through history, and who loves passionately to the point of becoming flesh (John 1). These were the glimpses of God that I was already getting when I wrote some of the journal entries that I have shared.

The essence of God is relational, directed to the other: the center of the belief in the Trinity is the communion between God and us. Jesus is the true union of the human and the divine. He is the medium for our individual communion with God and with each other. When we shift our reflection from the inner life of God to God-with-us, we see that the trinitarian doctrine has radical implications for Christian life.

God is revealed in creation, in the face of Jesus, and in the power of the Holy Spirit, who facilitates the communion between God and God's creatures. This is the only way to understand the Christian God. Moreover, we cannot understand ourselves unless we realize that, like the divine Persons, our vocation is to communion. We are called to live in communion with all creation and with one another in God.

But it is one thing to understand this in my head and another to have what some spiritual writers call a unitive experience. This happened when I was staying again in a hermitage in Erie, Pennsylvania, in 1986. I copy from my journal:

> *Journal*
> *April 12, 1986*
> *10:00 A.M.*
> *Hermitage in Erie*
>
> I walked into the woods. What an experience! I was not in control. The woods are foreign, unknown, dark at times, scary, and yet . . . what a wonderful feeling I get walking through the woods. It's a sweet combination of fear and joy; darkness when I only look to the trails; but what an awesome light if I dare look up to the sun shining timidly through the branches. I am sure they are also part of the face of God.
>
> I plunged into this mystery; be bigger than I am, let me live, move and have my being in you (cf. Acts 17:28).
>
> As I got out of the woods, I saw the ocean waiting for me. I went to it, and took off my sandals. . . . I am on holy ground! I collected rocks; and they spoke to me of the transcendence and immanence of God. Rocks are strong, they seem eternal, but they are so vulnerable when they are pushed against each other by countless waves.
>
> *"Philip, the Father (Creator) and I are one"*
> (John 10:30).

Does this mean that part of your "tremendous" being is changed by the impact of human waves like these rocks? Was your face affected by the spits and blood that covered the face of Jesus?

"Philip, whoever has seen me has seen the Father" (John 14:9).

As I read this journal entry, I realize that throughout my entire life I have been "searching" and "finding" the mystery we call God. I am also aware of the insights I have been given, sacred moments of union of the divine out-there with the divine within me. The Trinity is not a doctrine about God removed from all but a doctrine about God's life with us, and about our relationships with one another and with creation.

When God created the universe and life, God envisioned unity and established an order to reach it. When God created human beings, God also envisioned unity, but freely chosen. God wanted us to use our freedom to live in unity and in communion, open to each other and to the entire creation.

Teilhard de Chardin argued that the human condition necessarily leads to the psychic unity of humankind, and he also stressed that this unity can only be voluntary. He stated that "evolution is an ascent toward consciousness . . . and therefore signifies a continuous upsurge toward the *Omega Point*, which for all intents and purposes, is God."[7]

Unity in diversity does not mean uniformity. It means oneness, "That they may all be one" (John 17:21). This unity can take place in the midst of differences.

I live and minister in an extremely diverse area. I deal with personality differences, cultural differences, diversity even in the ways we image God. This is the richness of our world, and it reflects our God, who cannot be contained in any single image.

For me personally, the most frequent source of conflict in South Florida is the tension among Latinos, Haitians, and Euro-Americans. Everything we do is culturally determined. However, most of our programs are permeated with the values of the dominant culture. Mainline America is generally defined as a task-oriented culture, while Hispanic and Haitian cultures are usually designated as family-oriented. These differences cause conflict when we are planning religious events.

First of all, different cultures have different images of God. Culture is also about the way we think about God, how we feel about God, when and where and how often we relate to God. It is how we pray when we are alone and how we pray when we are together.

I have often planned liturgies in which the music and the symbols did not speak to Latinos or Haitians. Both of these cultures prefer a more lively music in church than the Euro-American, and they also enjoy staying after Mass simply to socialize. To imagine unity among people who have different images and experiences of God and opposite ways of celebrating life seems an impossible dream. And yet that is God's vision for the universe and Paul's hope for the Body of Christ.

The issues of isolation, individualism, and narcissism in our mainline culture today do not contribute to this communion and unity; the process of spiritual evolution requires a unification of consciousness. In the words of Teilhard de Chardin, "no evolutionary future awaits anyone except in association with everyone else."[8]

He coined the term "Omega Point" to describe the higher level of consciousness toward which the universe appears to be evolving and is the actual *cause* for the universe to grow. He was able to keep the Omega Point within the orthodox views of the Christian God, who is transcendent (independent) of his creation, but he also argued that the Omega Point resembled the "Word, namely Christ, who draws all things into himself and who is "God from God," "Light from Light," "True God from true God," and "through whom all things were made."

Displaced Longing

In the fourth century C.E., St. Augustine wrote in his *Confessions* the famous words, "You have made us for yourself, O Lord, and our hearts are restless until they rest in you" (1.1). We have an insatiable need for love that only God can satisfy, but since many do not know God, we try to fulfill our longing for God/Love through other objects of attachment. I call this idolatry, we turn people or things into gods, and they drain all our energies.

One of these idols is money or possessions. Many people, including Catholic Christians, are willing to do anything for wealth. In itself, wealth is not a problem, except when our possessions possess us and we become their slaves. What happens when my happiness and the healthy relationships in my family depend totally on the amount of money I make? What is wrong when I cannot share love with my spouse because the instability of the economy is eating me up? If I worry about my finances and try to be a responsible and wise investor, I am fine. But the moment that my fears and anxiety isolate me from my loved ones, then I am guilty of idolatry.

Perhaps the most dangerous "god" we worship is "human relationships." One of the basic human needs is the need to love and to be loved. This is our birth right. "God is love," and we have been created in God's image and likeness. Thus, we are also "love." The problem starts when we refuse to accept the limitations of human love. We seek perfection in human relationships and are disappointed when others do not love us the way we want to be loved. Actually, we are looking for God's love in our relationships, and so we place a tremendous burden on one another. We will never be loved in the way we desire and were created for. Even the most perfect relationship will always fall short of our needs and expectations.

Recently, a couple came to see me because of some marital difficulties. The husband was working three jobs to support his four children and wife so she could stay home. He usually left the house at 5:00 A.M. and returned exhausted around 11:00 P.M. After a shower and dinner, he was ready for a good night's sleep.

The wife wanted to share with him how the children were doing in school, how they were behaving, the latest developments in the little ones, and so on. She was totally frustrated because as soon as she started to talk, he would fall sleep. He, on the other hand, was complaining that she would not stop talking when he needed to sleep. The discussion went on for several minutes.

Finally, she looked at me and said, "Isn't he supposed to be my best friend, to make me happy and to help me with the children?" After an hour of heated conversation, I moved to affirm their mutual needs. He deserved his rest, and she deserved a friend who would listen. Unfortunately, reality was very different, and neither one was able to meet all the expectations of the other. I suggested that during the day she called a friend or her sister and share with them about the children or anything else that she wanted to talk about. I told him to make sure that at some point during his two days off, they took time to be with each other and to listen to each other. Eventually, they understood that their expectations of the relationship were unrealistic and that God was the only one who could give them the undivided love and attention they craved.

Situations like this are frequent, and they cause suffering in relationships. We become demanding, dependent, or overpossessive. What I find fascinating is that for the most part we do not understand that we are demanding perfection from others, perfection that we have the right to desire, but that only God can give us. "You have made us for yourself, O Lord, and our hearts are restless until they rest in you." Anything short of divinity will fail to satisfy us.

On the other hand, we usually do not believe that God's love is unconditional and infinite! How many times do we say, "God cannot love me that much, I don't deserve it!" Or, "How can God forgive me when I cannot forgive myself?" Something is wrong with this picture! We expect human beings to fulfill our every need, and yet we do not think that God is able or willing to do the same. This attitude speaks volumes about our image of God. We need to let God be God and humans be humans!

I could name many other "gods" that we worship in today's culture: power, sex, control, fame, to name just a few. When we expect these "gods" to quench our desire for love, we become obsessed, angry, anxious, self-centered, isolated, and above all, slaves of the idols we ourselves create. Some spiritual writers call this attitude, "displaced longing."

Christ became one of us to free us from alienation, narcissism, and stagnation, reminding us of the covenant relationship: "No one can serve two masters; for a slave will either hate the one and love the other, or be devoted to the one and despise the other. You cannot serve God and wealth" (Matthew 6:24). "Wealth" could be substituted for any of the idols I have already mentioned. This is one of the greatest challenges of our century, to have a clear image of the God we believe in and to reject the worship of false idols.

Who is God for the twenty-first century Christian? Is God limited to the human expression in Jesus of Nazareth over two thousand years ago? Does our image of God still reflect anger, revenge, and punishment outside the context of love and compassion that Jesus revealed?

I know that for many of us, our image of God justifies our behavior; I have seen this happen many times in myself and in others.

If I believe in a God who is trying to catch me off guard so that he can destroy me, I will probably think that I have the right to be the same way with others. In my experience, this happens frequently in work situations, where the boss thinks he has the right to be mean and authoritarian. (Try asking him or her who God is for them!)

If I have never experienced the forgiveness of God, it will be hard for me to forgive anyone. It has been said that we often make God in "our image and likeness," and sadly I believe this to be true. If I envision God as a gentle, loving father or mother who cannot stand conflict, I will probably act that way also.

I had a very sad experience in a local parish where an elderly lady served as cantor. She had had a beautiful voice as a young woman many years ago, but now she sounded more like a drunk, hysterical woman, screaming or competing with a cat for a singing prize. Everyone in the community was upset because her singing was really a distraction and actually a negative element in the liturgy.

As a representative of the archdiocese, I talked to the pastor about the situation. He agreed with everything I said but told me that asking her to stop singing was not "the Christian thing to do." I reminded him of his responsibility to the entire community that was being affected by the awful singing that did not help them to praise and pray. He reiterated his position and told me that the "good Lord" would have never done such a hurtful thing to a poor old lady. His misled compassion continued to hurt the community, and his own weakness and mistaken image of God supported his decision.

The Suffering God

Some Catholic thinkers appropriate the Greek understanding of the dualistic nature of God. For them, God is beyond time and space, incapable of suffering, inscrutable, and untouchable. They believe in a God totally removed from humanity. Although Catholic theology maintains the belief in God's intervention in human history, the attributes of immutability, impassibility, and so on, have always remained part of the conversation.

If God has no feelings, creation and incarnation make no sense, and the Bible is a book for fools. The pain, sadness, and even anger of God that we find in its pages reflect the depth of God's love for us; these profound emotions are expressions of God's pain in the face of our infidelity and indifference, and they prove how much God cares.

If God cannot suffer, then the sufferings of the Christ cannot be a genuine revelation of God. One of the errors of the first four centuries was that Jesus suffered in his humanity, not in his divinity, thus in effect making each nature an independent person. Consequently there is no real incarnation. If God is denied suffering, Christ's death would be the death of just another human being, not the death of the incarnate Word of God.

In Christ and through the Spirit, God is the loving presence, comfort, and strength in the face of evil and suffering. The Creator experiences our sufferings on a much deeper level than we could ever imagine. This is one of the most unknown or ignored truths about God in our Christian tradition. Most Christians do not accept a God who feels, suffers, or gets angry.

The emotion of anger has always interested me. After my father died, my mother processed her grief by getting angry. Her anger was displaced toward my brother and me, and often toward her own mother. Because of this and many other experiences with angry people, I decided to help others deal with this emotion. My main objective was to enable them to discover the presence of God in the midst of their anger.

I started by offering a retreat called "Finding God in My Anger." It was going to take place in a retreat house, and we advertised it all over the archdiocese. Soon I received a letter from the pastor of a local parish asking me to cancel that heretical event. In great detail and with kindness, he explained that anger was a "capital sin" and that God could not be present in it. First we had to be healed from our anger so that we could then find God in a holier, peaceful place.

I was furious and sad at the same time. How could a priest believe that there was a feeling or a place where God was not? In the words of the psalmist:

> *Where can I go from your spirit?*
> *Or where can I flee from your presence?*
> *If I ascend to heaven, you are there;*
> *if I make my bed in Sheol, you are there.*
> —Psalm 139:7-8

I wrote a letter explaining the retreat and encouraging him to pray about his feelings asking God what he was trying to tell him through them. With the letter I included copies of the handouts and notes that I used for the retreat. Of course, I went ahead with the program, and more have followed.

Many people have benefited from the experience and claim to have a deeper sense of inner freedom and to have discovered a new way of relating to God. I never heard from the priest again, but I still feel sad and remember him in my prayer often.

If God cannot suffer, grieve, or feel anger, can God love at all? Anyone who believes that God cannot suffer has to answer the question, "Can God love?"

There is a pervasive fear of change in all of us that includes even God. Somehow, the belief that God changes implies weakness, and therefore this God cannot be the true, unchangeable, impassible Christian God.

If we truly believe, with St. Paul, that Christ is the visible image of the invisible God, then Christ reveals a suffering God. Christ's heart is the heart of God, the heart of the universe. Thus, Christ's passion reveals the passion in the heart of God. But some scholars argue that the suffering of Christ does not necessarily mean the suffering of God. Can the impassible God experience suffering?

No traditional Christian doctrine has taken a greater bashing from modern theologians than the assertion that God is "impassible" by nature—that is, that he cannot experience suffering—because, they argue, a God who cannot suffer is completely insensitive, uninvolved. Dietrich Bonhoeffer wrote from prison, "Only the suffering God can help."[9] Additionally, one who cannot suffer cannot love either, and that would make God a loveless being.

Some theologians have solved the question by asserting that indeed God suffered in Christ. But for others, the sufferings of Christ happened in his human nature and did not touch the divine nature of the Creator Father. The classical view—and one that makes much sense—affirmed that Christ suffered, not that the Word of God did, for the divine, being without a body, is incapable of suffering.[10]

The concept of suffering at the time of early Christianity applied mainly to the body, and because God does not have a body, he cannot suffer. This challenges my previous statement that the incarnation is the only possible answer to the suffering of God. The flaw I see, and some early Fathers saw too, is that to them suffering was only physical; obviously, if God has no body, it is impossible for God to suffer.

This position contradicts my experience. I have suffered many physical illnesses in my life and emergency surgeries, but I can say without any doubt that none of them has been as bad as the psychological or spiritual suffering that I have endured: loss of loved ones, loss of country and friends, alienation, envy, and many others. Why should we limit the word "suffering" to just its physical expression?

I believe, as some theologians do today, that God can suffer in his divine nature and that the concept of suffering needs to be revisited.

Let me use as an example my experience with the Cuban Revolution and its impact in my personal life.

I mentioned before that my father died suddenly, but I did not add that the date was January 19, 1959, eighteen days after the triumph of the Castro Revolution. My mother was left with two children to raise on her own while she was also in the process of losing her vision.

About a year later, some members of the militia came to our home to tell my mother that they would be returning in a few weeks to take my twelve-year-old brother to join the Pioneers in Russia. My mother became hysterical and begged the men to spare my brother since she had just become a widow, and he was now "the man of the house." Of course, her pleas went unheeded, and they told her the date when they would be back for him. When my eighty-two-year-old grandmother tried to intervene, one of the men pushed her against a sofa and told her to stay out of the way. Thanks to a program sponsored by the Catholic Church in the United States and the American government (Peter Pan Program), my mother was able to send my brother alone to Miami to stay in a camp. My brother and I had never slept even one night away from home without our parents!

I saw my mother's and grandmother's suffering, their agony, and the despair my brother felt during those first days alone in a camp in the wilderness of South Florida.

After a few weeks, we received a letter from my brother. He was panic stricken and begged for me to join him. He had not taken a shower in weeks for fear of the wild animals in the Florida swamps. I joined him in Miami two months later. We were in two different camps but were able to speak on the phone and visit once a week. Right at that time, Castro closed the flights between Havana and Miami. Our family arrived four years later, and by then my brother and I became the "parents" and caregivers of four elderly women.

There was never any physical pain. None of us was beaten or tortured or gassed, but the suffering was beyond anything I can explain, especially for my mother and my brother. It made sense to ask whether they were alone in their suffering or if God participated in it. No one would ever be able to convince me that God was not suffering with us because of his impassibility. I strongly believe that God was in the midst of our suffering, our fear, and our anger, just as God is involved in every other aspect of creation.

If the Word became flesh to reveal the face of God, then the psychological, emotional, and even spiritual pain of Christ reflects the pain of God. Nearly every theologian and average Christian accept the image of a God whose nature is relational, who longs to be in an intimate relationship with each of us and who desires communion with all creation. We affirm that this is the description of the trinitarian God. How can we logically say that a God who loves, desires, and longs for us, who gets involved in our lives, is incapable of suffering when the beloved suffer?

Perhaps we can say that God is impassible not because he does not suffer but because no suffering could be strong enough to diminish or destroy God's love for us. This love will never change; that is God's impassibility!

There are many Scripture passages that confirm my belief in the suffering of God. I realize that a good exegesis must be done in order to understand fully the meaning of each one. Yet this task does not belong in this work. My intention is simply to highlight the message that the Spirit of God is revealing to us in the words of the sacred authors. The rest I leave to the biblical scholars.

In the Book of the prophet Micah, we find the following lament:

> *O my people, what have I done to you?*
> *In what have I wearied you? Answer me!*
>
> —Micah 6:3

To me these words reflect sadness and frustration. "Why do you repay my love with evil?" They do not seem to come from an impassible deity.

As I move away from the Hebrew Scriptures, I turn to Jesus' life and find much suffering.

> *Again he [Jesus] entered the synagogue, and a man was there who had a withered hand. They watched him to see whether he would cure him on the sabbath. . . . And he said to the man who had the withered hand, "Come forward." Then he said to them, "Is it lawful to do good or to do harm on the sabbath, to save life or to kill?" But they were silent. He looked around at them with anger; he was grieved at their hardness of heart and said to the*

man, "Stretch out your hand." He stretched it out, and his hand was restored.

—Mark 3:1-5

Jesus was misunderstood, doubted, ridiculed, and angry. But the difference between his anger and ours is that he used his to do good. The energies of the emotion of anger did not cause any harm to the Jews, but healed the man. Can we still argue that Jesus, the icon of God, did not feel anything?

In the Letter to the Philippians (c. 57-58 C.E.), Paul praises the congregation, teaches, encourages, admonishes, and warns, but always with a clear love for the members. He asks the community to look to the interests of others and to have the same mind that was in Christ Jesus,

who, though he was in the form of God,
did not regard equality with God
as something to be exploited,
but emptied himself,
taking the form of a slave,
being born in human likeness.

—Philippians 2:6-7

This christological statement implies that the suffering of Christ is not limited to his passion and death. In his human state, Jesus felt every possible emotion. He was rejected, betrayed, misunderstood, laughed at, and finally murdered. Christ's suffering and, with it, the suffering of God embrace the whole world and the lives of everyone in it. There is no love without suffering, and God is and always will be love.

The anger and contempt that some people feel toward God are as old as humanity. The cause is the conviction that all evil comes from God and that he should be held accountable for his actions. What follows may seem funny, but it clearly shows the degree of hatred toward God that some feel even today:

> *Nebraska Senator Sues God to Stop Terror Threats,* by Ryan Singel, September 17, 2007.
>
> Nebraska State Senator Ernie Chambers (D–Omaha) filed suit against God Friday, asking a court to order the Almighty and his followers to stop making terrorist threats. The suit filed in a Nebraska district court, contends that God, along with his followers of all persuasions, "has made and continues to make terroristic threats of grave harm to innumerable persons."
>
> Chambers, in a fit of alliteration, also accuses God of causing "fearsome floods, egregious earthquakes, horrendous hurricanes, terrifying tornadoes, pestilential plagues, ferocious famines, devastating droughts, genocidal wars, birth defects, and the like."
>
> Likewise the suit accuses God of having his chroniclers "disseminate in written form, said admissions, throughout the Earth in order to inspire fear, dread, anxiety, terror and uncertainty, in order to coerce obedience to Defendant's will."[11]

Some will laugh and dismiss this article as a joke. Far from it, I think it reflects the relativism and atheism of our society today. In many circles, including the political arena, God has become a joke. More than ever we need a good theodicy that honestly confronts the goodness of God and the mystery of evil. The next chapter will be devoted to this topic.

In the meantime, I will end this section with a description of the God I believe in. Once, a long time ago, I complained to a friend that I was always searching and that it was tiresome. She wisely replied that I was also always finding and that was rewarding. This has proven true. I will forever be searching and finding new and fresh experiences of God in my own journey. What follows is my present understanding of God.

Creator and Creation Are Dynamic

Teilhard de Chardin saw creation as a process; "it has never ceased. Its act is a great continuous movement spread out over the totality of time. It is still going on; incessantly but imperceptibly the world emerges more and more from nothingness."[12]

This is my concept of God and creation, dynamic, always happening, in process, centered in the Word, the Omega Point, and the cosmic Christ. Christ combines God's dynamic, creative Word and preexistent Wisdom as the instrument of God's creative activity, the fulfillment of creation. I believe that ours is a dynamic creation and that God, rather than being immutable, is always happening!

This is the only way that I can accept the coexistence of God and evil. We are growing, we are suffering growing pains, but there is also hope because God is with us. Yes,

"It" happens, but the God of my faith and my experience is fully immersed in "It."

The God I believe in

- is the Creator of the cosmos and of everything that is and will be;
- has the capacity to relate and communicate because God's essence is love;
- is the totality and the source of the energies of love;
- in mysterious and inexplicable ways, desires to be in communion with creation;
- took on humanity to show that there was no difference between the sacred and the secular, between Creator and creation;
- is the God in whom I live, move, and have my being;
- suffers with my sufferings and rejoices with my joys;
- waits patiently and actively assists me to realize my full potential;
- welcomed my Mason father into his heaven because he was God's beloved son.

All around us, to right and left, in front and behind, above and below, we have only to go a little beyond the frontier of sensible appearances in order to see the divine welling up and showing through. But it is not only close to us, in front of us, that the divine presence has revealed itself. It has sprung up universally, and we find ourselves so surrounded and transfixed by it, that there is no room left to fall down and adore it, even within ourselves.

By means of all created things, without exception, the divine assails us, penetrates us and moulds us . . . the world, this palpable world, which we were wont to treat with the boredom and disrespect with which we habitually regard places with no sacred association for us, is in truth a holy place, and we did not know it. *Venite, adoremus.*[13]

Chapter 3

The Mystery of Evil

Do not be overcome by evil,
but overcome evil with good.
—Romans 12:21

Evil is ultimately a mystery, just as love and life are mysteries also. We know they exist, we feel them, we experience their activity within and among us, but we can never fully grasp their essence. Every theological explanation for the existence of evil in a good universe created by a good God is merely a feeble attempt to ease our human need to know and understand mystery.

No one denies that there is something desperately wrong with our world; we only have to watch the news, look around, or simply be alive. To struggle with the apparent contradiction between the existence of evil and the belief in a good God is perhaps the most crucial challenge for all of us.

Evil is the greatest obstacle to believing and trusting in God. As theologian Hans Küng has said, suffering or evil is "the acid test" for every religion.[1]

We know that mysteries are not problems to be solved, but we cannot ignore or deny their existence, particularly in the case of the mystery of evil. We must continue to probe and explore its meaning especially for the sake of those who suffer its effects.

In religious tradition, evil has been explained primarily as the consequence of original sin, the sin resulting from the fall of Adam and Eve due to an act of disobedience to God that cost them their intimacy with God and their life in paradise. Some see it as the punishment of an angry and vengeful God or a test to help us become better persons. It is common to hear, "God is testing my faith!" For others, evil is the logical outcome of personal and social sin, actions that go against the order and the goodness of creation. Many see Satan, the "prince of lies," as the cause of all evil. Still others dismiss the whole concept as a puzzle or a mystery that is not meant to be explored. Finally, among radical Christian fundamentalists, there are a few who pay more attention to the power of darkness than to the light and spend their energies trying to plan strategies that will help win the battle between the two forces.

Whatever the explanation, sooner or later the questions appear: Why did God allow this to happen? If God knew, why did God not prevent it? And so it goes.

What is the best theodicy that can be offered to those who honestly search for answers?

God in the Prophetic Literature of the Bible

I begin with the thwarted images of God that we have inherited. There is the common misconception that the

God of the Old Testament, the God of Israel, is a God of anger, punishment, and revenge. The study of biblical criticism and the analysis of these writings in their social and historical contexts are beyond the scope of this book. Nevertheless, I can point out that God's acts of justice, wrath, or punishment found in the pages of the Hebrew Scriptures, are always contained within God's love and mercy. Every apparent evil attributed to God is meant not to punish, but ultimately to restore a broken relationship.

The Book of the prophet Hosea, one of my favorites, is a good example. Hosea gives little information about his life. The "oracles" reveal "a very sensitive, emotional man who could pass quickly from violent anger to the deepest tenderness. The prophecy pivots around . . . the painful experience he underwent in his married life."[2]

Hosea's wife, the adulteress, symbolizes Israel and her unfaithful relationship to God, and just as Hosea could not give up his wife forever, so God could not renounce Israel in spite of her idolatry and her oppression of the poor, both violations of the covenant. "God would chastise, but it would be the chastisement of the jealous lover, longing to bring back the beloved to the fresh and pure joy of their first love."[3]

God's love for us has never been expressed more tenderly in spite of a context of pain and anger. Hosea/God says,

Therefore I will hedge up her way with thorns;
and I will build a wall against her,
so that she cannot find her paths.
She shall pursue her lovers,
but not overtake them;
and she shall seek them,
but shall not find them.

Then she shall say, "I will go
and return to my first husband,
for it was better with me then than now."
She did not know
that it was I who gave her
the grain, the wine, and the oil,
and who lavished upon her silver
and gold that they used for Baal. . . .
Now I will uncover her shame
in the sight of her lovers,
and no one shall rescue her out of my hand. . . .
Therefore, I will now allure her,
and bring her into the wilderness,
and speak tenderly to her. . . .
There she shall respond as in the days of her youth, . . .

On that day, says the LORD, you will call me, "My husband," . . . I will make for you a covenant on that day . . . and I will make you lie down in safety. And I will take you for my wife forever; I will take you for my wife in righteousness and in justice, in steadfast love, and in mercy. I will take you for my wife in faithfulness; and you shall know the LORD.

—Hosea 2:6-20

The Book of Hosea is the first to describe the relationship between God and Israel as a marriage, a symbolism that will appear again later in the Old Testament. Hosea's seemingly unkind acts are meant to bring his wife back, all his mean actions have just one purpose: to show his wife, Gomer, that she was falling for false lovers and that he, Hosea, was her true love and the one who really cared for her forever.

The central message of the Hebrew Scriptures is that God heals all our diseases, crowns us with steadfast love and mercy, and satisfies us with good as long as we live. God works vindication and justice for all who are oppressed. God is merciful and gracious; slow to anger and abounding in steadfast love. Our God does not deal with us according to our sins, nor repay us according to our iniquities. As far as the east is from the west, so far he removes our transgressions from us (cf. Psalm 103). We can say that when evil deeds occur, they are usually caused by people's behavior, and not random acts of a capricious deity.

Old Testament writings reveal a God who cares for the people and who desires to be in a covenant relationship with them. Every time they break the covenant, God intervenes through the prophets to call them back to him. God's will is for the healing of suffering and the overcoming of evil.

> *Learn to do good;*
> *seek justice,*
> *rescue the oppressed,*
> *defend the orphan,*
> *plead for the widow.*
>
> —Isaiah 1:17

Isaiah is considered the greatest of the prophets, and he lived during a critical period of Israel's history (the second half of the eighth century B.C.E.). He had a deep awareness of human sinfulness and was overwhelmed by the abyss between God's goodness and holiness and humanity's sin.

The ministry of Isaiah may be divided into three periods, covering the years 742 to 687 B.C.E. Little is known about the prophet's last days, but his oracles constantly reminded his wayward people of the fidelity of God to the covenant. Although the book was written mainly by the prophet, many of his disciples, deeply influenced by him, wrote some of the latter parts. Isaiah 56-66 was written in a later period by those who continued the work of the prophet. It is from this "Third Isaiah" that I offer a reflection.

Chapter 58 deals directly with God's expectations from the people in fulfillment of the covenant. The words demonstrate once again God's desire for the good of the people. It was a classic predicament: they were complaining to God because their prayers and fasting were not being heard. Isaiah's oracle (the words of God) was strong and challenging.

God says unambiguously through the prophet:

Tell my people their wickedness . . . and their sins . . .
They ask me to declare what is due them . . .
"Why do we fast, and you do not see it?"
Lo, on your fast day you carry out your own pursuits,
and drive all your laborers.
Yes, your fast ends in quarreling and fighting . . .
Do you call this a fast,
a day acceptable to the LORD?
This, rather, is the fasting that I wish:
releasing those bound unjustly,
untying the thongs of the yoke;
Setting free the oppressed,
breaking every yoke;
Sharing your bread with the hungry,
sheltering the oppressed and the homeless;

Clothing the naked when you see them,
and not turning your back on your own.
Then your light shall break forth like the dawn,
and your wound shall quickly be healed . . .
Then you shall call, and the LORD will answer,
you shall cry for help, and he will say: Here I am!
If you remove from your midst oppression,
false accusation and malicious speech;
If you bestow your bread on the hungry
and satisfy the afflicted;
Then light shall rise for you in the darkness . . .
Then the LORD will guide you always
and . . . renew your strength.

—Isaiah 58:1-11, NAB

Are these the words of a God who wishes suffering and evil upon the people? Do they reflect feelings of revenge and hatred?

What I hear is the sadness of a mother or father who has graced her or his children with marvelous gifts and has given them every possible opportunity to become the best they can be. Instead, they are selfish; they quarrel, ignore one another's needs, and yet continue to demand the attention of the parents.

God's words in the Old Testament are reproachful but not hateful. God gives them another opportunity, reminding them that if you care for each other, if you remove oppression and injustice from your midst, if you treat everyone justly, then light shall rise for you in the darkness.

Can we honestly say that this God is responsible for the evil in the world? Could it not be that we are using God as a scapegoat to avoid facing the part that all of us play in the "sad" condition of our world today?

Still, evil remains the most serious objection to the existence of a good God.

Interestingly, any explanation we offer for the existence of evil and suffering in the world is very subjective. Evil can be seen as good depending on the eyes of the beholder. The following story is almost unbelievable; it tells about two families who drew opposite conclusions from the same situation.

God the "Thief"

When I was a teenager, my three-year-old cousin died of leukemia. I still remember her little head covered with huge bumps that made her sweet face look distorted. After a long period of suffering, she died. Her parents, especially her mother, were inconsolable. Weeks after the funeral, she would still cry asking why God had allowed this evil to happen to her sweet baby.

With the best of intentions, someone told her that she should be happy, because now she had an angel in heaven watching over the family and that it was an honor that God had chosen her little girl when God needed an angel. The mother went crazy and threw the lady out of her home.

From that moment on, she stopped going to church and refused to let anyone speak about this monstrous God who stole little happy children when he needed more angels in heaven. This happened a long time ago, and it was not until two or three years ago that my cousin began to go back to Church and reconciled herself with God.

In training pastoral ministers, I always use this story as an example of what can happen when we offer stupid answers to very complex questions. I encourage my students to be a presence for grieving people and to refrain from engaging in theological discourse. Participants always see the wisdom of the story and take my recommendations at face value. *Mea culpa!* How wrong can one be in thinking that one has the answers for everything! Recently, I was the keynote speaker at a national ministry conference. I had been asked to speak about grief and to offer suggestions to the pastoral ministers who accompany people during the grieving process. As I prepared for my talk, I was grateful to have had the experience of my cousin's passing and hoped to be able to share it with them, something I resolutely did. At the end of my presentation, a young couple approached me to thank me for my words and then proceeded to share their own story.

Two years earlier, they had been in a terrible car accident caused by a drunk driver. Their twin children were in the back seat of the car. Sadly, they did not survive the crash and died on impact. I offered them my condolences and assured them of my prayers. I asked them if there was anything I could do for them. With beatific smiles they both told me that I had already done enough, because I had confirmed that their babies were little angels in heaven. They did not merit such a gift: to have their beautiful twins living happily as angels watching over them and interceding for them in the presence of God!

I thought I was hallucinating! They had misinterpreted the story and heard exactly the opposite of what I had said. My words, which basically discouraged their position, had served to convince them that they were right! Something was definitely wrong with this picture! For a long time I was speechless. Should I tell them how wrong their image of God was? Should I explain that God does not kill little children when there is a shortage of angels in heaven? By the grace of God, I remained silent. They hugged me and with tears in their eyes thanked me for the gift I had given them that afternoon.

Was I wrong? Does God kill little children because there is a need of angels in heaven? Was the couple spiritualizing their loss and creating a terrific defense mechanism to cope with the pain? Should I have talked to them about my image of God, the God who welcomed my Mason father into eternity?

That day I learned something new. God, evil, and suffering are very real, but they are interpreted, integrated, and experienced in different ways according to each person and his or her particular context. Does that mean that I should not be writing on these topics? On the contrary, that experience affirmed even more the need to create safe and sacred spaces where people can share their ideas, feelings, and beliefs on these existential issues.

Original Sin

Traditionally, most Christians accept the doctrine of original sin to explain evil and suffering and let God off the hook. The doctrine itself is not easy to understand; for centuries, theologians and philosophers tried to come up with a reasonable way to explain it.

In the fourth century, Augustine of Hippo was responsible for the concept of original sin as the "root of all evils."

The basic foundation of original sin from the Augustinian perspective is that God exists and is good; therefore, God would be incapable of creating evil. Something else, then, must be its source. The fall of our first parents (original sin) offers an explanation for all the wrongs that happen to us and to the world today.

I have never related to this teaching, and it does not offer me any consolation when I have to deal with what I call "the power of darkness." The gift of a free will given by a good God to a good creation could only bring about good choices and would not imply "freedom" to do evil unless God gave us a flawed free will, and that makes no sense to me either. To infer that we, "perfect creatures," created in the image of God and living in paradise, ruined a perfectly good creation by abusing our free will is absurd. I know people who "choose evil," but it is often because their natural inclination toward good has been hindered by some psychological or sociological problem. Their so called freedom has been damaged by circumstances. Maybe I am naïve, but I am totally in agreement with Anne Frank who from her small hiding place in Amsterdam wrote in her diary:

> Everyone has inside of him a piece of good news. The good news is that you don't know how great you can be! How much you can love! What you can accomplish! And what your potential is!

She also believed, as I do, that, "despite everything, people are really good at heart."[4]

Indeed, for those of us who believe in the basic goodness of people as creations of a good God, the doctrine of original sin as we have been teaching it for centuries does not hold a candle to the question of evil. For me, a good and acceptable explanation was given by St. Irenaeus (second century), considered the most modern of the early Fathers of the Church. In an age when evolutionary theories did not exist and everyone used the doctrine of the fall to explain evil, Irenaeus affirmed that the Son had come not only to save the fallen, but to advance them on the way toward the heights of divinization.[5] He held that free will is a gift from God, but his understanding of this freedom varied from the common explanations we hear in our churches and catechetical settings. Irenaeus believed that freedom did not mean that people were "totally and completely" free when they sinned against God according to the mythological account found in Genesis. He noted that human beings had the "potential" and the "call" to be more, to develop and evolve, but in their beginning stage, they chose what they already had and gave up the possibilities that awaited them. In an act of supreme pride, which continues today, they attempted to become gods without God.

I do not call this sin "original" but immature and self-centered. The children in my family are blessed to have everything they need, but that does not prevent them from asking for a toy that belongs to another child and that they already have sitting in their closet. The first word that my little grandnephew spoke was, "mine!" Is this caused by some great sin sexually transmitted from generation to generation in an inexplicable way? I rather believe that he likes the sound of the word, and it makes him feel good; he is asserting himself and telling the world, "I am here, I am a person, and this toy belongs to me!"

We often have to take the time to teach children and guide their actions, gradually to help them become aware that they are not the center of the universe and that there is a world full of people around them. Am I oversimplifying a tough question or avoiding the true answer? Fortunately, I am not alone in my thinking.

For Irenaeus, creation is like a divine pedagogy. Human beings are meant to be perfected by God in time. They are taught by God what it means to be human, moment by moment, not all at once. "Thus, in the beginning of history, they are not developed or complete. Their origins are primitive even though they are destined for growth."[6]

This second-century idea sounds revolutionary and could scandalize Christians even today when most assume that human beings were "perfect" at the moment of creation. Irenaeus definitely had an evolutionary view of creation, and to me that is awesome!

He visualized primitive humans as young beings looking forward to the future, and their sins were nothing other than growing pains. He believed that "paradise, in a way, was less in the past than in the future. The history of man is not that of a laborious ascent after a vertical fall, but a providential progress towards a future that is full of promise."[7]

In his *Proof of the Apostolic Preaching*, discovered at the beginning of the twentieth century, Irenaeus agrees with Augustine's concept that humans revolted against God's commands, but for him that revolt "resembles more the caprice of a child than the pride of a devil."[8]

> If the origin of evil is free will, and God is the origin of free will, isn't God then the origin of evil? Only as parents are the origin of the misdeeds their children commit by being the origin of their children. God gave us a share in his power to choose freely.

> Would we prefer he had not and had made us robots rather than human beings?[9]

Today, evolution is accepted by every scientist even though they do not agree on the various theories. We would make a terrible mistake if we viewed the Genesis account according to a static worldview.

Irenaeus's vision, like that of Teilhard de Chardin, gives me hope, encouragement, and even certain anticipation. I believe that God's universe is not imperfect or flawed, but slowly moving toward its fulfillment. Christ points to the future of the cosmos, and this helps me to make some sense of my own sufferings and those of the world around me.

This universe has a destiny; the world will not be destroyed. Rather, it will be brought to the conclusion that God intended for it from the "beginning, which is anticipated in the mystery of the Incarnate Word and glorified Christ."[10]

According to traditional doctrine, any explanation of evil must include the goodness and omnipotence of God, human free will, and suffering as the consequence of the willful turning away from God. I think that the words of both Irenaeus and Teilhard honor these three elements but from a more evolutionary and optimistic perspective. I believe in the goodness of God and in free will as they do, and I do not accept the concept of the fall of "perfectly good" individuals who lived in paradise, communing intimately with the Creator every day (cf. Genesis 1:31).

Later on, in the thirteenth century, St. Thomas Aquinas shed more light on the topic. For him, "evil is neither an essence nor a nature nor a form nor an act of being—evil is an absence of being; it is not a mere negation, but a privation: the privation of a good that should be in a thing."[11] This does not mean that evil does not exist, but that it has to exist in good, the good that is intrinsic to the creatures of God. Thus, there is no positive source of evil connected to God.

All realities are in themselves good; therefore, evil becomes efficacious not by itself, but through the wound that it inflicts on the good. The power of evil is the very power of the good it damages. The more powerful this good is, the more powerful evil will be.

Let us take greed as an example. Greed in itself has no power unless it preys on people who are talented and who are in the position to promote the common good. The evil power of greed depends on how much it damages the power of good innate in each person. In other words, evil feeds on goodness. We could conclude that without good, there can be no evil.

In this respect, Irenaeus offers another insight. "Temptation, sin, and suffering are necessary conditions if egoistic humans are to become loving persons. . . . God could eliminate evil, but at the price of creating unheroic humanity, a race of pampered children. God is powerful enough to spoil humans, but too wise and good to do so."[12]

I believe that this is the same thing we do with our children. We can certainly "force" them to study so they can get good grades, but the growth will not happen until they decide on their own to become the best students they can be. Parents who allow their children to get everything without any effort are actually creating a race of losers and underachievers. When we overspoil our children, we are not really loving them, but enabling and encouraging in them harmful patterns of behavior.

Do I dare say that a world without evil would be a good place, but it would not be the best place possible? It seems to me that, paradoxically, good and evil need to coexist so that our world is not only "good," but "very good." God not only wanted free creatures; God also wanted loving relationships, communion, plenitude—that is, the greatest good possible.

God did not make a world of perfect computerized robots, but one in which true moral development is possible in persons whose character is formed through growth and struggle. Certain virtues could not exist without suffering or evil: patience, compassion, forgiveness, peacemaking, nonviolence and faithfulness, to name a few.

I know that I am a better person because of what some consider evil. My father's sudden death, our exile from our country of birth, my mother's blindness, my little cousin's leukemia, the struggles to finish graduate school, my many illnesses since I was young, the humiliations, the financial crises, and so on, are all experiences that have made me the person I am today. I believe that the greatest good that has come out of these "evils" is the ability to empathize with someone else's pain and to walk in their shoes, to be a woman of hope, to enjoy and share a great sense of humor, and to believe without any doubt in the goodness of God and of the universe.

The Tempter

Also known as the devil, Lucifer, Satan, and the Prince of Darkness and lies, the Tempter plays a central role in the mystery of evil. The *Catechism of the Catholic Church* explains it this way:

> The Church teaches that Satan was at first a good angel, made by God: "The devil and the other

demons were indeed created naturally good by God, but they became evil by their own doing." Scripture witnesses to the disastrous influence of the one Jesus calls "a murderer from the beginning," who would even try to divert Jesus from the mission received from his Father.[13]

Evil is not an abstraction, but refers to a person, Satan, the Evil One, the angel who opposes God.[14]

The devil's main weapon against man is temptation. The devil normally doesn't take people on directly, he simply introduces a thought or object to them, hoping to begin a dialogue. *We must never dialogue with temptation.*[15]

In the Gospel of Mark, we find an excellent example of the Tempter's role in the classic dialogue between Peter and Jesus. On one occasion when Jesus was walking with his disciples, he asked them, "Who do people say that I am?" After a variety of answers, Jesus insisted, "But who do you say that I am?" Peter answered him, "You are the Messiah."

> *Then Jesus began to teach them about his passion, death and resurrection. Peter took him aside and began to rebuke him. But turning and looking at his disciples, Jesus rebuked Peter and said, "Get behind me, Satan! For you are setting your mind not on divine things but on human things."*
>
> —Mark 8:27-33

In the parallel version in the Gospel of Matthew, Peter rebuked him, saying,

> *"God forbid it, Lord! This must never happen to you." But Jesus turned and said to Peter, "Get behind me, Satan! You are a stumbling block to me; for you are setting your mind not on divine things but on human things."*
>
> —Matthew 16:21-23

Peter's refusal to accept Jesus' prediction of his suffering and death is seen as a satanic attempt to deflect Jesus from his God-appointed course, and the disciple is addressed in terms that recall Jesus' dismissal of the devil in the temptation account (Matthew 4:10): "*Get away, Satan*!" (NAB).[16]

This harsh treatment of Peter, calling him Satan, challenges all believers to total commitment to Jesus through acceptance of the cross of suffering. Jesus recognizes in Peter the voice of the Tempter using Peter's weakest point—fear—as we will see later after the arrest of Jesus when Peter hides and denies Jesus three times.

There are many references to the devil and demons in the Scriptures. The classic passage to illustrate the devil's presence and action is the story of the temptations of Jesus in the desert. According to the Gospels of Matthew and Luke, Jesus, full of the Holy Spirit, was led by the same Spirit into the wilderness to be tempted by the devil. It seems contradictory that Jesus "full of the Spirit" was taken by the same Spirit to encounter the devil. The logical expectation would be that if one is full of the Spirit, he or she would have nothing to do with the devil. Yet Jesus faced the enemy after fasting for many days, and he was challenged to command a stone to become a loaf of bread. He answered with the famous words "One does not live by bread alone." Then the devil promised him power and glory if Jesus would worship him. Jesus answered with another verse from the Scriptures. Finally, the devil took him to Jerusalem and asked him to prove that he was the Son of God by jumping from the pinnacle of the temple. For the third and last time Jesus refused to give in. Then the devil left him until an opportune time (cf. Luke 4:1-13).

There is no contradiction in the story. Jesus can face the devil precisely because he is filled with the Holy Spirit. The exchange concludes in Jerusalem, the city where Jesus will ultimately face his destiny. Although apparently Jesus "won" the battle, the Gospel tells us that the devil would return at the opportune time, namely, before Jesus' passion and death.

Some scholars question the literal accuracy and historicity of the three temptations. In my opinion, they are missing the point. I believe that the evangelists are actually telling our own stories and incorporating them into that of Jesus to make the One Story—the story of our own lives torn between good and evil.

I have never seen the devil, but I have experienced the three temptations at different times throughout my life. I have desired power, control, prestige, and security in my struggle between the power of darkness and the power of light. I have heard the whispers of the Tempter without ever seeing him. Surprisingly, I do not have any entries on evil as such in any of my journals.

My experiences with evil are very different from those with God and suffering. I have never seen the face of evil, but I can sense its presence. I intuit evil more than I "see" it. My favorite phrase to describe it is, "the power of darkness," which I borrowed from a drama by Leo Tolstoy, and from the Gospel of John: "The light shines in the darkness, and the darkness did not overcome it" (John 1:5).

I could be listening to a person during a spiritual guidance session and feel the darkness, I can almost see it and smell it. I seldom think that the person is evil, but rather that the power of darkness is using this person in the weakest area of his or her personality.

I also sense the difference between mental illness and evil. It is impossible to explain, but I have experienced it over and over for more than thirty years in the ministry of spiritual guidance. I have shared this with other people in the same ministry, and some have had similar experiences.

There are also evil situations and evil structures, but I do not see them as possessed by demons or by Satan. Sometimes I go somewhere, and I have to leave immediately because I sense the darkness in the room. It feels as if a lot of sinfulness and godlessness had occurred in that place.

When it comes to structures and institutions, I believe that centuries of sin have made them evil or sinful. If we take the example of the institutional dimension of the Catholic Church, I can say that I have experienced its evil during more than thirty years of professional lay ecclesial ministry. In my opinion, the evil resides not in a few cases of pedophilia but in the centuries of infidelity to God and to the Gospel on the part of the institution and some of its religious leaders.

These infidelities have many causes: some are political and social; others are financial and historical; but at the root of all evils is greed and a demonic desire for power. Most of the individuals that have been the main actors in these evil performances were people deeply affected by all the circumstances I mentioned before but who were not necessarily evil themselves.

We could call it "the sin of the world," a condition that touches and wounds all of us. This condition has a double cause: the imperfection of the still growing and developing universe and the accumulation of all the sins of humanity, particularly arrogance, egotism, greed, and infidelity to God.

On the other hand, when we look at the history of any institution, we also find moments of grace. In my years ministering in the Church, I certainly saw sin, but I also saw grace, "where sin increased, grace abounded all the more" (Romans 5:20). I have known real saints who are not on the altars, people who draw their energy and joy from their relationship with God. They are also people of faith, who trust in the promise and look forward to its fulfillment. All of us are born with the basic needs for power and control, esteem and affection, and security and survival. When these centers begin to control us and we start idolizing them, we can say that the "power of darkness" has won.

Similarly, Jesus was tempted throughout his entire life. The Letter to the Hebrews says, "we have one who in every respect has been tempted as we are, yet without sin" (4:15). "Because he himself was tested by what he suffered, he is able to help those who are being tested" (2:18).

We need to be vigilant and aware of the allurements of the power of darkness, but we must also remember that we are not dealing with two deities of equal power. The Catholic belief is clear: "The power of Satan is not infinite. He is only a creature. . . . He cannot prevent the building up of God's reign."[17]

During a Bible class in one of the local parishes, I had divided the participants into small groups. As I walked around the room, I overheard a discussion about soldiers and armies. I asked what they were doing, because it had nothing to do with the class, which was about the Prologue of the Gospel of John. Their answer was unbelievable. Using some passages from the Books of Kings and the Book of Revelation, they were trying to figure out how many "soldiers" were in the two armies that were going to be fighting for the earth in Armageddon.

This was one of the days when I decided not to teach Bible in parishes anymore!

There was no need for me to say anything, because the class members were convinced that I took Satan and Armageddon very lightly and did not understand the tremendous power he had, so much so that Jesus ended up hanging on a cross. According to them, this final battle was going to determine the future of the world: Christ versus Satan!

> *In the beginning was the Word, and the Word was with God, and the Word was God. . . . All things came into being through him, and without him not one thing came into being. What has come into being in him was life, and the life was the light of all people. The light shines in the darkness, and the darkness did not overcome it.*
>
> —John 1:1-5

The most difficult issue to deal with when we talk about evil is hell. Does hell not contradict the existence of a loving and compassionate God, the God who welcomed a Mason into heaven? Actually, there is no contradiction, because hell is the consequence of free will. We choose hell; God does not cast anyone into hell against one's will. If a creature is really free to say yes or no to the Creator's offer of love, then it must be possible for the creature to say no. Free will, in turn, was created out of God's love. Therefore, hell is a result of God's love. Everything is. No sane person wants hell to exist. No sane person wants evil to exist. If there is evil and if there is eternity, there can be hell.[18]

The Church has always maintained that hell is not so much about fire and heat as about the absence of God. If we go back for a moment to my remarks on idolatry and false gods in our society, it will be easier to understand the concept.

Before his passion, Jesus prayed, "Father, the hour has come; glorify your Son . . . since you have given him authority . . . to give eternal life to all whom you have given him. And this is eternal life, that they may know you, the only true God, and Jesus Christ whom you have sent" (John 17:1-3). Therefore, the Gospel tells us that eternal life is not "pie in the sky" or something that happens only after our death. Eternal life is to know God and Jesus the Christ; it is to have a personal loving relationship with God that translates into love and compassion toward our brothers and sisters. If this is the choice we make in life, this will be our heaven for all eternity but to a degree that we are unable to imagine now.

On the other hand, if my god has consistently been money, and if that is the idol that I worship, I will spend my eternity "cherishing" it. Often the extreme love of money jeopardizes family relationships, friends, and concern for the common good. If money has made me greedy, with no concern for the suffering of others, that is my choice. Even before I die, I have chosen how I will spend eternity. That lonely eternity, loveless and surrounded by money, is hell!

In the New Testament we find a parable that gives us an idea of who, according to Jesus, had chosen hell. The parable of the rich man and Lazarus (Luke 16:19-31) illustrates Luke's attitude toward the rich and the poor and also the teachings of Jesus in the "Sermon on the Plain": "Blessed are you who are poor, for the kingdom of God is yours. Blessed are you who are now hungry, for you will be satisfied. Blessed are you who are now weeping, for you will laugh" (Luke 6:20-38).

Jesus turned around the values of his time. The ones he called blessed were the poor, the hungry, the suffering. Similarly in Matthew 25, at the last judgment, those who went to hell were precisely the ones who failed to help the least ones:

> *For I was hungry and you gave me no food, I was thirsty and you gave me no drink, a stranger and you gave me no welcome. . . . Then they will answer and say, "Lord, when did we see you hungry or thirsty . . . and not minister to your needs?" He will answer them, "Amen, I say to you, what you did not do for one of these least ones, you did not do for me."*
>
> —Matthew 25:42-45

Jesus blessed the poor, and maybe we do not consider ourselves poor—but everyone is poor in one area or another. Maybe our poverty is fear, and it is there that we will find God.

According to the *Catechism of the Catholic Church,* "The state of definitive self-exclusion from communion with God and the blessed is called 'hell.' . . . The chief punishment of hell is eternal separation from God, in whom alone we can possess the life and happiness for which we were created and for which we long."[19]

One Example of Social Evil

I hesitate to call "evil" those actions caused by sins or human flaws. Yet there is a social phenomenon in our culture today that, for some reason, I cannot call social sin. I experience it as "evil." I am referring to "noise."

When I looked up the meaning of the word in the Merriam-Webster Dictionary Online, I was both shocked and affirmed in my opinion about this "evil."

- *Noise. Noun*: loud, confused, or senseless shouting or outcry.
- A sound; *especially* a: one that lacks agreeable musical quality or is noticeably unpleasant; *b*: any sound that is undesired or interferes with one's hearing of something; *c*: an unwanted signal or a disturbance (as static or a variation of voltage) in an electronic device or instrument (as radio or television); *broadly*: a disturbance interfering with the operation of a usually mechanical device or system.
- *Origin of the word noise.* Middle English, from Anglo-French, disturbance, noise, from Latin *nausea*. First known use: 13th century.
- *Synonyms*: Babel, blare, bluster, bowwow, brawl, cacophony, chatter, clamor, clangor, discordance, rattle, roar.
- *Antonyms*: Quiet, silence, still, stillness.

- *Noise pollution*: annoying or harmful noise (as of automobiles or jet airplanes) in an environment.

Everything that I want to say about this "evil" is summarized in these definitions, but I want to spend some time reflecting on this topic. I love music; I do not mind some noise; I fly a lot, and the noise in the planes does not bother me. I can be surrounded by all six little ones in my family, ranging from one to nine years old, and I actually enjoy their screams and loud noises.

This is not the kind of noise I am talking about. When I speak about the evil of noise, I mean the noise that prevents us from listening to one another, from hearing the cry of the poor and the pleas of widows and orphans. It is the noise that silences the voice of God and the song of the birds, the heartbeat of a loved one, and the last breath of a dying friend.

The causes of this evil are multiple, diverse, and subtle. When Teilhard de Chardin spoke about the transformation of consciousness and the development of humanity, he added a fear of his: the pace at which technology, science, and other disciplines were developing could not be compared to the slow and hesitant spiritual development of the human consciousness.

I once watched on television a Senate hearing on cloning. The two members appearing before the Senate were a Greek scientist advocating cloning and a ethicist presenting the dangers and ethical issues involved in this scientific development. It was embarrassing! The level of knowledge and preparedness, the presentation, the ability to communicate the pluses of cloning left the ethicist looking like a child who had joined the baseball game in the seventh inning. The only thing he said that made some sense was, "The fact that we have the knowledge and the ability to do something, does not mean that we should do it." These are wise words that I have heard many times and that even I, in my ignorance, could have added to the conversation.

We only have to watch the news or most of the television programs to realize that the most watched are the noisier ones. I have friends who have walked out of a theater in the middle of a movie because the film was boring—it had no action, too many silent moments, and the pace was slow. Entertainment has turned into episodes of noise pollution, and any complaint indicates that you are a bitter, old person who should stay home watching silent movies.

Then there are cell phones, iPods, MP3 players, Blackberries, and CD players; we also spend hours texting and so on. I admire this technology and of course have a cell phone. They are good, helpful for business, and entertaining. Like anything else, the problem begins when we become addicted to them. When these objects that were created to make our lives better become idols, we are possessed by them. I know people, especially young persons, who are plugged in to their iPods twenty-four/seven. They do not talk to each other and when they want to communicate, they text. This way of communicating, especially in couples, avoids disagreements and conflict as well as intimacy.

I do not think it is necessary to give more examples. Everyone knows what I am talking about, but I want to recall something that I wrote in the section on *the Tempter*,

"Jesus recognizes in Peter the voice of the Tempter using Peter's weakest point: fear."

What is one of the weakest points in our culture today? I believe fear is definitely controlling many people. We are afraid of losing our jobs, our homes, our pensions, and our Social Security payments. We are afraid of getting sick because we do not have health insurance. We are afraid of international and domestic terrorism, of natural catastrophes, and of apocalyptic cataclysms. We fear because we have lost out trust in the government, in the school system, in the medical profession, even in religious leaders. We want to block everything and escape from our fears. Among other things, noise can do that. If I combine noise with drugs or alcohol, even better. We are living in the age of despair.

Many have said that our times need hope above all else. True, but I do not think that we are able to hear that message with all the noise in our lives. It is in this context that I believe noise is a social evil. Politicians have proven that: they talk the talk, but they do not walk the walk, and when they do, nobody is listening anymore.

I do not blame Apple, or Sony, or any other corporation for the noise, but I think that the evil of greed lurking in the background has a lot to do with it. To me, this is more than the accumulation of individual sins. The power of darkness is behind this social illness in ways that I cannot explain.

Yet I do not feel hopeless. I am the eternal idealistic and optimistic person knowing that God will bring some good out of this mess. There are signs coming from all corners of the earth calling us to spiritual growth and calling us to leave our comfort zone and move toward a deeper level of consciousness. Spiritual writers and scientists are beginning to use a similar language, and many people are responding. That gives me hope!

> *Be still, and know that I am God!*
>
> —Psalm 46:10

> *Then the word of the LORD came to him [Elijah]. . . . He said, "Go out and stand on the mountain before the LORD, for the LORD is about to pass by." Now there was a great wind, so strong that it was splitting mountains and breaking rocks in pieces before the LORD, but the LORD was not in the wind; and after the wind an earthquake, but the LORD was not in the earthquake; and after the earthquake a fire, but the LORD was not in the fire; and after the fire a sound of sheer silence. When Elijah heard it, he wrapped his face in his mantle and went out and stood at the entrance of the cave. Then there came a voice to him.*
>
> —1 Kings 19:9-13

Individual and Social Sin

> *I will sprinkle clean water upon you, and you shall be clean. . . . A new heart I will give you, and a new spirit I will put within you; and I will remove from your body the heart of stone and give you a heart of flesh.*
>
> —Ezekiel 36:25-26

"God is Love" (1 John 4:16), and the energy of love is the source of all life. Therefore, when people turn away from

God, they lose the capacity to love and to live. Sin is breaking the intimacy with God.

Since I do not accept a dualistic view of the world or of the person, when I speak about sin I refer to our spiritual and physical separation from God. Body and spirit are one in the whole human being. If one dimension of the person suffers, the entire person suffers. When I have a severe headache, I put my entire body to bed—why, if only my head hurts?

When we rebel against God spiritually, our bodies also suffer the consequences. St. Paul writes a very strong letter to the Christian community in Corinth. He admonishes them because when they come together as a church, there are divisions among them. In truth, they do not gather to eat the Lord's Supper because each goes ahead with their own supper, and one goes hungry and another becomes drunk.

With angry words, Paul tells them that they are showing contempt for the church of God and humiliating those who have nothing. His final words are rather harsh: "Examine yourselves, and only then eat of the bread and drink of the cup. For all who eat and drink without discerning the body, eat and drink judgment against themselves. For this reason many of you are weak and ill, and some have died" (1 Corinthians 11:28-30).

I do not think that Paul is implying that God makes people sick or kills them if they fail to behave properly when they celebrate the Lord's Supper. But, as I said earlier, I believe in the unity of the person, and I know that when I am physically ill, especially in a lot of pain, my spiritual life is affected. Likewise, when sin affects my spiritual body, my physical body suffers. God does not have to punish me with an illness; I bring it upon myself; I am simply unhealthy and spiritually dehydrated. Whether I am dealing with resentment or anger, or with guilt for the offense committed, I will be anxious and nervous, and my body will suffer the consequences. I believe this is what Paul meant in his message to the Corinthians.

I once treated a lady on the mental health floor who was unable to walk because of the burden of unhealthy guilt. She was married to a Christian minister who wanted sex and at the same time considered it dirty. His reason for the negative part of sex was a sick understanding of some of the biblical rules about menstruation. He though that his wife was always "unclean," and he forced her to wash herself with rubbing alcohol before intercourse.

Somehow the wife had tolerated this situation for over a year, but finally she could not put up with the physical pain and the psychological abuse any longer. Unable to refuse her husband's request because she felt compelled to be the faithful and valiant woman of the Bible, she "lost" all feeling from the waist down and became paralyzed. Many doctors saw her and decided that there was nothing physically wrong with her; they sent her to the mental health unit, where she arrived in a wheelchair.

Her husband was constantly by her side "praying for healing" and promising eternal love. The more he kept up this behavior, the worse her condition got. She was consumed by guilt, and the only defense or way out she had from her "Christian wife duties" was to be paralyzed.

Individual sin is a selfish choice made by one person. If someone else is hurt, the harm is a direct consequence of my actions. St. John is very clear when he says,

> *This is the message we have heard from him and proclaim to you, that God is light and in him there is no darkness at all. . . . If we walk in the light as he himself is in the light, we have fellowship with one another. . . . If we say that we have no sin, we deceive ourselves, and the truth is not in us. If we confess our sins, he who is faithful and just will forgive us our sins and cleanse us.*
>
> —1 John 1:5-10

We may try to fool ourselves, but we know when we have sinned against God, ourselves, or others; we are also familiar with the disease deep in our hearts. Everyone accepts the notion of sin, and even when we do not admit it publicly, we know something is not well with us.

On the other hand, what we call social sin is more complicated. Social sin is collective, an aspect of our society that is not congruent with the reign of God or with the good news of the Gospel.

In his Apostolic Exhortation *Reconciliation and Penance,* Pope John Paul II gives an excellent definition of personal and social sin:

> Sin, in the proper sense, is always a personal act, since it is an act of freedom on the part of an individual person. . . . But it is a truth of faith, also confirmed by our experience and reason, that the human person is free. This truth cannot be disregarded in order to place the blame for individuals' sins on external factors such as structures, systems or other people. . . .
>
> Social Sin. To speak of social sin means in the first place to recognize that, by virtue of human

solidarity . . . each individual's sin in some way affects others . . . there is no sin, not even the most intimate and secret one, the most strictly individual one, that exclusively concerns the person committing it. With greater or lesser violence, with greater or lesser harm, every sin has repercussions on the entire ecclesial body and the whole human family . . . every sin can undoubtedly be considered as social sin.

Some sins . . . constitute a direct attack . . . against one's brother or sister. . . . Likewise, the term social applies to every sin against justice in interpersonal relationships, committed either by the individual against the community or by the community against the individual. Also social is every sin against the rights of the human person . . . social is every sin against others' freedom, especially against the supreme freedom to believe in God and adore him; social is every sin against the dignity and honor of one's neighbor. Also social is every sin against the common good and its exigencies in relation to the whole broad spectrum of the rights and duties of citizens. . . .

Social sin also refers to the relationships between the various human communities. . . . Thus the class struggle . . . is a social evil. Likewise obstinate confrontation between blocs of nations, between one nation and another, between different groups within the same nation, all this too is a social evil. . . .

Whenever the church speaks of situations of sin or when she condemns as social sins certain situations . . . she knows and she proclaims that such

> cases of social sin are the result of the accumulation and concentration of many personal sins. It is a case of the very personal sins of those who cause or support evil or who exploit it; of those who are in a position to avoid, eliminate or at least limit certain social evils but who fail to do so out of laziness, fear or the conspiracy of silence, through secret complicity or indifference; of those who take refuge in the supposed impossibility of changing the world. . . . The real responsibility, then, lies with individuals. At the heart of every situation of sin are always to be found sinful people.[20]

War is an excellent example of social sin and the personal responsibility involved in it. When the United States was planning the war against Iraq, Pope John Paul II made very radical public declarations:

> POPE WARNS AGAINST WAR
>
> VATICAN CITY (CNS) — Pope John Paul II spoke out against a possible war against Iraq, telling Vatican-accredited diplomats that military force always must be "the very last option," even when motivated by legitimate concerns.
>
> In an annual "state of the world" address Jan. 13, the pope said the future of humanity depends partly on the earth's peoples and their leaders having the courage to say "no to war."
>
> "War is not always inevitable. It is always a defeat for humanity," he said.

> "And what are we to say of the threat of a war which could strike the people of Iraq, the land of the prophets, a people already sorely tried by more than 12 years of embargo?" he said. . . .
>
> In recent weeks, a growing chorus of Vatican officials has warned against resolving the Iraqi disarmament problem through war, pointedly rejecting the notion of a "preventative war" in the case of Iraq. . . .
>
> Reviewing the world situation at the start of 2003, the pope said he had been "personally struck by the feeling of fear which often dwells in the hearts of our contemporaries."
>
> "Never as at the beginning of this millennium has humanity felt how precarious is the world which it has shaped," he said. "Yet everything can change," he added. *"It depends on each of us."*[21]

The conflict and disagreement between the Holy Father and President George W. Bush and other world leaders were obvious. Inserting the Vatican opinion at this point is not a political issue. Rather, it goes to show what I mean by social sin. At the time, the majority of the Catholics I know disagreed with the pope. The aftermath of 9/11 created a culture of fear dominated by feelings of retaliation and violence.

The pope was simply reiterating the principles of a "just war" promoted by the Church's social teachings for decades. I heard many comments opposing his view and alleging that he was too old and sick and that his mind was not clear. These are the same pro-life Catholics who oppose abortion and euthanasia but perhaps approve of capital punishment. The decision to invade Iraq was made, and we are all living its consequences. We still have many different opinions on the subject, but let us not forget that at a very critical point of our history the pope's position was ignored.

Today, we do not talk much about it, but war remains a social issue. Let us remember the pope's words: "Never as at the beginning of this millennium has humanity felt how precarious is the world which it has shaped. Yet everything can change. It depends on each of us." Destructive or positive consequences flow indirectly as a cumulative result of all the different individual choices.

> I have seen war. I have seen war on land and sea. I have seen blood running from the wounded. I have seen men coughing out their gassed lungs. I have seen the dead in the mud. I have seen cities destroyed. . . . I have seen children starving. I have seen the agony of mothers and wives. I hate war.
>
> —Franklin D. Roosevelt, address at Chautauqua, New York, August 14, 1936

Another example of social sin is the life that some institutions, systems and structures can develop and that eventually turns into a life of their own. Their crimes against the common good go beyond the accumulation of the sins of their members. At some point, this "life" grows and develops in spite of the conversion and good intentions of each individual.

Conversion, the change of heart from evil to God is possible in the human heart; but can a system convert? Can the heart of stone of most of our institutions, religious included, be changed into a heart of flesh? Many advocate for systemic or structural change only to discover that there are just a few examples of such "miracles" in our history books. It is easy to understand why mainstream Christianity focuses on individual rather than social sin. Social sin is the cause of many evils in society and is almost impossible to identify and to solve.

As I have already said, we are always looking for scapegoats. What better way to divert the blame than to hold the school systems, the welfare systems, the religious structures, or the governments responsible for all the ills of the world? True, they have developed a life of their own, but it is also true that we still have power to effect change and cannot continue to play the "Pontius Pilate game!"

Many years working in the religious system have taught me that I can never completely change it. Yet I have many examples of moments when either my colleagues or myself took a strong position and "forced" the powers that be to alter a decision. Most of them had to do with budget matters. As a staff, we had to defend in front of the financial board the need to continue training the laity for ministry. Usually those who serve in finances are removed from the pastoral life of the Church. We could have simply acquiesced and obeyed their decision to cut our budget, but we clearly saw that it was an issue of justice to defend our position. We did, and they reversed their decision.

Jesus knew what we would have to face when he said, "See, I am sending you out like sheep into the midst of wolves; so be wise as serpents and innocent as doves" (Matthew 10:16). This wise advice applies not only to the Church but also to any other institution that we attempt to change. The wisdom or shrewdness of serpents is indispensable, because systems not only have power over their members, but can also destroy those who attempt to redeem them.

An Example of a "Minor" yet Powerful Social Sin

A few years ago, I was on my way to teach a class to a group of lay ministers. The parish where the gathering was held was about sixty miles from my home. I took the Florida Turnpike in order to get there faster. As soon as I started the trip, I remembered that I had not eaten anything since breakfast, and this meeting was probably going to last until 11:00 P.M. I decided to stop in one of the rest areas and get something to eat.

I entered the shop and picked up a turkey sandwich, a diet soda, and a muffin. During the time I was choosing my food, there was a man, poorly dressed, maybe homeless, who did not look too friendly to me. Since I travel a lot at night, I am usually cautious around strangers. Muggings are common in South Florida. I kept an eye on the man, but he never got close to me.

By the time we got to the cashier to pay, he had a muffin and a coffee in his hands. Since I had taken longer to choose my food, he was ahead of me in the line. When he gave his items to the lady she told him, "It's $7.25." The man asked, "So much money for just coffee and a muffin?" "Sorry," she answered, "that's what it is." The man gave her the muffin, and asked, "How much for just the coffee?" "$2.75," she said. "OK then, I'll only take the coffee." He paid and left.

I placed my sandwich, muffin, and diet soda on the counter, and paid the astronomical amount, while the lady said, “They should check how much money they have before they make me waste my time!”

Suddenly, I had an epiphany. I looked at all the food I was getting and realized that it never occurred to me to pay for the man’s muffin. I felt my heart jumping in my chest with the awareness of my indifference and lack of compassion. I picked up my stuff without even getting the change and ran outside to look for the man. He was gone, nowhere to be seen. I do not mean to dramatize the moment, but it was dark outside and honestly, he had no place to go. I knew immediately that I had just seen Christ hungry and had not given him anything to eat!

Finally, I arrived at the church and started my class. I rudely stopped in the middle of my presentation and shared with them what had happened on the way and my feelings about it. It was an amazing and sad experience. Everyone began excusing me for not helping the man: “I had to be careful being a woman alone; one never knows when the person is a criminal.” “This ‘kind’ of man would have used my money for booze.” When I insisted on sharing my sadness and the fact that I knew I had “missed the mark,” they proceeded to give me a speech about the social conditions in the area and how it was not “my” fault that we had so many homeless around. The government should be doing “something.”

I still remember my level of frustration. I had sinned against God, my neighbor, and the Gospel, and no one would accept it. We were all Catholics. True, my sin was individual, but my contribution to poverty, a social sin, was very real!

We usually accept racism, genocide, oppression of the poor, and violations of human rights as social sins. Yet I believe that when I failed to pay for the man's food I also contributed to the social sin of poverty. When John wrote the Prologue to his Gospel, he was not talking about an afterthought invented as an answer for original sin. We are grateful and awed because from the beginning God knew that our faulty steps and growing mistakes were to be taken up by Christ, the beginning and the end of all creative processes, the Omega Point, the human face of the invisible God.

"From the beginning" means from the time of the Big Bang fourteen to fifteen billion years ago. Blessed John Duns Scotus, a priest in the Order of Friars Minor, the Franciscans, was one of the most important and influential philosopher-theologians of the High Middle Ages. "Scotus believed that the first idea in the mind of God was the Christ."[22]

My belief in the Cosmic Christ, the Word, the Omega Point, who was with God from the beginning, who is God, and for whom all things were made, makes the goodness of God easier to grasp and the hope for my own divinization real. "The incarnation is the renewal and the restoral of all the forces and the powers of the universe; Christ is the instrument, the Center, the Term of *all* creation . . . : by Him, everything is created, sanctified, vivified."[23] This tells me that I had no excuse for failing to see Christ in that homeless man even if I could not solve the homeless situation in our country. It also tells me that God was in "IT" and not "out there." If I can stop blaming others and instead focus on God in the midst of "IT," my hope is reborn.

If just a few of us would stay in "IT" long enough to clearly see God in the homeless man, together we would rediscover the energies of Love. "Someday, after mastering the winds, the waves, the tides and gravity, we shall harness for God the energies of love, and then, for a second time in the history of the world, man will have discovered fire."[24] I do believe that only God's radical involvement in human pain can make the goodness of God credible in a world seemingly gripped by evil. But we are the face of God in the world, and it is through our actions that all will see God's love manifested in their lives. Each one of us has a part to play!

My nine-year-old grandnephew made his First Holy Communion a year ago. Obviously, he also experienced his first confession. As time went by, he noticed that his mother, my niece, never seemed to go to confession. One day, he asked her, "Mama, why don't you ever go to confession? It is a very good thing. When I go, I tell the priest my little flaws. I know they are not big (pushing my sister, ignoring you when you call me). I know they are not horrible sins, but I want to be better, and when the priest forgives me in the name of God, I feel as if a heavy burden has lifted from my shoulders. Mama, I think you should try it; it will be good for you!"

Sometime after this conversation, my niece went to confession. When the priest asked her, "How long has it been since your last confession?" she answered, "about fifteen years." The priest then asked, "And what brings you to the sacrament today?" With a big smile she said, "My son!" Both of them are wonderful, good people, and in my opinion, neither one needed to go to confession. Yet something wonderful happened that day: a child was saying, "I want to be good, and, Mama, I want you to be good also." This was a simple example of a mother and her child saying "no" to sin and "yes" to the loving God revealed by Jesus.

Remembering this event puts a smile in my heart and makes me hope that many people would be willing to follow the request of a child. I know that for some it is difficult to move from sin to freedom. Maybe the issues discussed in the next chapter can explain some of the reasons.

Chapter 4

Understanding Anger and Forgiveness

Be angry but do not sin;
do not let the sun go down on your anger.
—Ephesians 4:26

Recently I was meeting with a woman for spiritual guidance. She was having great difficulty letting go of a particularly painful memory. She wanted to let go, but for some reason she continued to cling to it almost neurotically. I suggested welcoming her feelings as brothers and sisters, trying to see God in them and hear what God might be saying to her. She thought that made a lot of sense and promised to try it.

When I offer retreats on anger or forgiveness, the hardest part is helping people to see that, as long as they do not embrace their pain, the energies in the strong emotions of anger and in the inability to forgive will end up controlling them. It is not unusual to hear someone say, "He is out of control," and that is exactly what happens when we allow those energies to control our feelings and behavior.

Energy is energy, and it does not have a moral connotation. I can transform the energy present in anger into a positive energy to heal and effect change. In one of my retreats, a woman approached me during a break and asked, "Are you trying to tell me that I have to forgive my 'ex'?" She was furious, literally out of control and yelling at me. As calmly as I could, I answered, "Of course not. I am not telling you what to do." I then asked her, "How long were you married?" She yelled, "Ten years! Married to this idiot, abusive man who had no respect for me, he was unfaithful, etc." "How long have you been divorced?" I said. Yelling even louder, she said, "Fifteen years!"

I hope that what I said next was inspired by the Holy Spirit and not by my sick sense of humor, but my words were, "This jerk made your life miserable for ten years when you were married, and now you are giving him fifteen more free of charge so that he can continue to ruin your life?" She seemed to be coming out of a trance and said, "O my God, you are right. He is living in California with his new wife and does not even think about me, and here I am, giving him all this power!" Her facial expression changed, her tone of voice became gentle, and she kept repeating how stupid she had been all those years, hoping that her hatred and ill wishes would kill him. By the end of the retreat, she had decided to put all her formerly wasted energies into helping herself and maybe going to professional counseling. Saint Jeanne de Chantal said it better: "Must you continue to be your own cross? No matter which way God leads you, you change everything into bitterness by constantly brooding over everything. For the love of God, replace all this self-scrutiny with a pure and simple glance at God's goodness."[1]

The truth is that the more you try to avoid suffering, the more you suffer because the fear of suffering becomes an obsession and controls your life. The same process happens with anger and the inability to forgive. As emotions go, they can easily cause bitterness, illnesses, sin, and of course deep suffering that often interferes with the individual and the communal well-being. They also offer attractive "cracks in our spiritual lives" for evil to sneak in.

Understanding Forgiveness

"Then Peter came and said to him, 'Lord, if another member of the church sins against me, how often I should forgive? As many as seven times?' Jesus said to him, 'Not seven times, but, I tell you, seventy-seven times" (Matthew 18:21-22). Forgiveness is the process of letting go of resentment, hatred, or anger as a result of a perceived offense, and of the need for punishment or restitution. The *Oxford English Dictionary* defines forgiveness as "to grant free pardon and to give up all claim on account of an offense or debt." Forgiveness is one of the most important Christian qualities, one of the most difficult to put into practice, and perhaps the most misunderstood.

The New Testament is rich in examples of situations where Jesus forgives someone. For the most part, the action scandalizes the audience, particularly the religious leaders.

- When Jesus saw their faith, he said to the paralytic, "Son, your sins are forgiven." Now some of the scribes were sitting there, questioning in their hearts, "Why does this fellow speak in this way? It is blasphemy! Who can forgive sins but God alone?" (Mark 2:5-7)

- "Her sins, which were many, have been forgiven; hence she has shown great love. But the one to whom little is forgiven, loves little." Then he said to her, "Your sins are forgiven." But those who were at the table with him began to say among themselves, "Who is this who even forgives sins?" And he said to the woman, "Your faith has saved you; go in peace." (Luke 7:47-50)
- "Whenever you stand praying, forgive, if you have anything against anyone; so that your Father in heaven may also forgive you your trespasses." (Mark 11:25)

When we choose to forgive others, we release ourselves from the power of sin. The act of forgiving then allows God to heal us in the context of that specific situation. Forgiveness can take place in five different contexts:

1. Accepting God's forgiveness
2. Forgiving ourselves
3. Asking to be forgiven
4. Forgiving God
5. Forgiving others (people, communities, institutions)

Accepting God's forgiveness is not easy, and it is very much connected with the inability to forgive ourselves. Most of us still believe that we have to "earn" or "deserve"

God's love and forgiveness. This goes back to the images of God I mentioned earlier in this book. If I do not believe in a God who is love and who longs to be in an intimate relationship with me, how can I believe in God's forgiveness? If I have never experienced forgiveness in my family, particularly from my father—and I see God as Father—it will be very hard for me to accept this free forgiveness. Many of us have been taught that we need to please God and be good, so that God will love us. We do not realize that we want to please God and be good as a response to the love that God already has for us.

Some time ago, I met a young woman who had two abortions when she was very young. She was suffering a lot now that she realized what she had done. She felt separated from God, depressed, and guilty. After several meetings, I ventured to ask if she wanted to go to confession. To my surprise she said, "I have gone twice, and the last time father told me that I did not have to confess the same sin again and that God had forgiven me." After a pause, I asked her, "Do you believe that God has forgiven you?" She said, "How can God forgive me when I cannot forgive myself?" We continued to pray and talk, and finally I realized that her feelings were not of guilt, but of grief! She knew the goodness of God, but she could not accept the fact that she had lost two children. We changed the direction of the conversation and started talking about how much she would have loved to have her two children now that she was older. I do not think this is an unusual or extreme case, but I know that situations like this can be very confusing to the person carrying the guilt and to those trying to help her or him.

At this point, my father, the lost son, the Samaritan woman, the woman caught in adultery, the man born blind, and many others come to mind, and I know beyond a reasonable doubt that God has forgiven them. I often wonder if our reluctance to accept God's forgiveness or to forgive ourselves is a sign of pride. Maybe we ask, "How can God forgive me if I have not done anything to deserve it?" Or, "Even if God forgives me I cannot forgive myself!" In the first case we are implying that we need to "buy or earn" God's forgiveness. In the second case we claim to know better than God. Do these questions sound like pride? They do to me.

The third context is when we need to be forgiven. I will not spend much time on this one, because I believe that this only takes an act of the will. If you know that you have hurt someone, ask for forgiveness. Period. End of story. There is not much to be said about this particular situation. It is the Christian way, and there are no gimmicks for it. Just do it! "So when you are offering your gift at the altar, if you remember that your brother or sister has something against you, leave your gift there before the altar and go; first be reconciled to your brother or sister, and then come and offer your gift" (Matthew 5:23-24).

When I bring up the fourth area of forgiveness, some people get upset with me. "What do you mean by forgiving God?" "How can you imply that God has done anything wrong?" I remind them that it was they who asked, "Why did God do this to me?" "Why did God make us free when he knew we were going to abuse our freedom?" and on and on. I list for them all the things that supposedly God has done to me: my father's early death, exile, illnesses, my mother's blindness, and everything else. Immediately they realize that, at one point or another, they have also asked similar questions.

There is nothing wrong with complaining to God. Everyone in the Bible did it, Jesus included. St. Teresa of Avila defined prayer as a conversation between two friends. The psalmists obviously agreed when they complained,

Why, O LORD, do you stand far off?
Why do you hide yourself in times of trouble?
—Psalm 10:1

Vindicate me, O God, and defend my cause
against an ungodly people . . .
For you are the God in whom I take refuge;
why have you cast me off?
Why must I walk about mournfully
because of the oppression of the enemy?
—Psalm 43:1-2

It is appropriate for us to demand answers from God. We might not get any that satisfy us, but at least a conversation is allowed. As Teresa said, these are two friends talking, and if I feel that my friend has let me down, I will let him know:

My God, my God, why have you forsaken me?
Why are you so far from helping me, from the words of my groaning?
O my God, I cry by day, but you do not answer;
and by night, but find no rest.
—Psalm 22:1-2

Even Jesus prayed this Psalm on the cross!

We often make the mistake of thinking that prayer has to be nice, comfortable, and sanitized. Jesus' prayer was honest, from the heart, real, and at times messy!

The final area in our reflection on forgiveness is forgiving others. This is the most misunderstood area. For example,

- Forgiving is not forgetting! We all know people who get into abusive relationships, but in a year we find them in the same situation. If we forget, we will never learn anything from our mistakes! When we have been deeply hurt, we never forget, but the wound is more like an old scar than a bleeding ulcer.

  When we forgive, we take away the power from the memory to continue hurting us. We do not let the old tape play over and over in our heads making our life miserable.
- I forgive even if the offending party has not asked for it or does not even want my forgiveness. Actually, I do not even have to let him or her know that I have forgiven them.
- Forgiving frees me from the burden and toxicity of angry feelings.
- Forgiveness does not mean that the offense was right or that I excuse it. It simply means that I will not allow the memory to destroy me.
- There are evil and destructive behaviors that are inexcusable: fraud, emotional and physical abuse, economic exploitation, human trafficking, racism, or any violation of human rights. Such actions cannot be excused or tolerated; they are evil and sinful. But even in situations

like these, we try to let go of our hatred. Otherwise, we are taking poison in the hope that it will kill the offenders.

- Forgiveness and reconciliation are not the same. This is a major source of conflict. We can forgive an abusive partner without having to go back to live with him or her. Forgiveness does not mean putting ourselves in dangerous or harmful situations.

  As Christians, we are called to forgive always, but we need to remember that forgiveness is a one-way street. Reconciliation, on the other hand, is a two-way street; the other person or community must be willing and able to change also. Forgiveness will always feel incomplete if it does not lead to reconciliation.

  I frequently hear people wondering if they have really forgiven, because the relationship with the other person is not healed. They do not feel happy with the outcome of the process, and they assume that their forgiveness was not real. For example, I can forgive my husband who has been abusing me for years, but I cannot be reconciled with him because he is unable or unwilling to change. Yet my forgiveness is real.

  If we think about the last hours of Jesus hanging on the cross, we will realize how radical forgiveness is and what the true meaning of reconciliation is.

  Two others also, who were criminals, were led away to be put to death with him. When they came to the place that is called The

> *Skull, they crucified Jesus there with the criminals, one on his right and one on his left. Then Jesus said, "Father, forgive them; for they do not know what they are doing." . . . One of the criminals who were hanged there kept deriding him and saying, "Are you not the Messiah? Save yourself and us!" But the other rebuked him, saying, "Do you not fear God, since you are under the same sentence of condemnation? And we indeed have been condemned justly, for we are getting what we deserve for our deeds, but this man has done nothing wrong." Then he said, "Jesus, remember me when you come into your kingdom." He replied, "Truly I tell you, today you will be with me in Paradise."*
>
> —Luke 23:32-34, 39-43

When Jesus asked his Father to forgive his murderers, he extended his hand to everyone. One of the thieves rejected his offer and kept on making fun of him while the other acknowledged his sins and grabbed Jesus' hand by means of a simple request, "Jesus, remember me." The forgiveness was valid in both cases, but reconciliation took place with just one of them. Moreover, when Jesus asked his Father to "forgive them," no one was asking to be forgiven; actually they were making fun of him and insulting him. Yet Jesus' act of forgiveness was not in response to a petition. He forgave because of who he was: the human face of the forgiving God.

- Forgiveness is a choice to move away from a place of pain to a place of healing and new beginnings.

- The inability or unwillingness to forgive eventually becomes its own kind of hell!
- Forgiveness is a process. Healing takes time; it cannot be rushed.
- For the process of forgiveness to work, we need to pray, pray, pray, and use all the energies that were wasted in hating into healing ourselves. "I came that they may have life, and have it abundantly" (John 10:10).

The struggle to forgive and the process of forgiveness give and take a lot of energy from us. Yet there is one other emotion loaded with energy that we usually label as negative. It is anger.

There are a lot of angry people in our world today. The social conditions are dire, and the pervasive impotence and hopelessness lead to anger. Unfortunately, the energy of this powerful emotion is seldom used in a positive manner. Anger is considered a negative emotion, a sin, a sign of mental problems or immaturity. In the context of God and suffering, it is necessary to take a good look at this misunderstood potential source of positive energy.

Understanding Anger[2]

Feelings are important tools to know ourselves. They point out situations that cause us pleasure or pain so that we learn to distinguish how our environment and relationships affect us. Yet most people are uncomfortable with their feelings, especially when they are considered negative. "In themselves passions are neither good nor evil.

Passions are morally good when they contribute to a good action, evil in the opposite case. Emotions and feelings can be taken up into the virtues or perverted by the vices."[3] We need to avoid placing any value judgment on our feelings and take them for what they are: signals that tell us that something is wrong in our lives or our health. Why do we treat anger differently?

When people refer to anger as a negative emotion, they are thinking not about the feeling, but about the violent acts or words that we see and that can be the manifestation of poorly handled anger. If we have been raised in the Christian tradition, we have been taught that certain emotions "should not" be welcomed. Our consciousness has been programmed by parents, by clergy, and by society in general to believe that "we should not feel this or that." Yet the important thing is not what we feel, but what we do with our feelings and how we express them.

Anger ranks at the top of the list of those emotions that are labeled "negative" or even "sinful." Oftentimes as children we were scolded for being angry. This meant being punished for our display of negative or destructive behavior. I believe this was the case of the priest who got so upset about my retreat on anger because this emotion appears on the list of capital sins. Yet there is a difference between the emotion of anger and the sin of anger. The Letter to the Ephesians tells us, "Be angry, but do not sin. The sun must not go down on your anger" (4:26). In other words, do not fear the feeling, but do not give it power to make you violent. Learn how to deal with it in a positive manner.

Anger is a reaction to our frustration because our ideas or expectations are not being satisfied. Most people have countless ideas about the way people or things "should be."

We expect a lot from our spouses, friends, children, parents, job, and church, even from ourselves. This is normal and even desirable. The problem is that more often than not we encounter a wide gap between our expectations and reality. This gap causes a frustration that varies in degrees depending on the severity of the gap and the importance of the ideal.

Imagine this situation: You enter a supermarket to pick up some lunch on your way to work. You not only find a long line, but the person in front of you does not have a valid ID card to show the cashier. She calls the manager who, of course, is busy in another part of the store. The light above the register continues to blink as you feel your blood beginning to boil. You are frustrated and rightly so. In normal circumstances, this feeling is temporary and disappears as soon as the inconvenience is resolved. Nothing to worry about! When this frustration is caused by serious abuses, injustices, or betrayal, or when it is experienced repeatedly, eventually it will turn into anger. At that point, the intensity of the feeling has surpassed that of a simple, occasional inconvenience.

There is no evil intention in anger. In itself, it is only a medium to deliver a message. My anger is notifying me that I need to pay attention to my frustration, which has gone unattended for some time. Many Christians are afraid of this feeling; therefore they do not pay attention to it. When anger goes unattended, it results in violence. Violence is anger turned into aggression inwardly or outwardly directed.

Outward directed aggression. Perhaps the most easily identifiable form of aggression is physical violence. When we see someone hitting someone else, banging their fists against the wall, throwing or breaking things, we surmise that they are angry. Actually, they are beyond anger and into its unhealthy expression, which I am calling aggression or violence. It is this manifestation, along with verbal abuse, that has given anger its bad reputation.

Verbal abuse includes screaming at others and insulting or diminishing them with our words and gestures. This is also an unhealthy way of dealing with anger. Gossip is perhaps the least recognizable form of violence. Because it does not include yelling or external aggressive behavior, it tends to be accepted as part of the human condition. Gossip is as violent as hitting someone. We use our tongue to destroy a person's reputation behind his or her back. By tarnishing someone's image and raising suspicion about his or her conduct, we think we are getting even. Gossip is unhealthy and does not do anyone any good.

Other forms of violence are passive and more difficult to identify. The most common is accurately called passive aggression. Passive aggression is a learned behavior that keeps a person from expressing anger in a healthy manner. The passive aggressive person is an angry, spiteful person who outwardly appears friendly, kind, and caring. Passive-aggressive behavior is a form of covert abuse. Covert abuse is subtle and veiled or disguised by actions that appear to be normal, at times loving and caring. The passive-aggressive person is a master at covert abuse.

Alongside passive aggression are silence and indifference, which are subtle ways to "hurt" others without becoming overtly violent. The "cold shoulder treatment," the "I am sorry, but I forgot," and persistent tardiness are insidious ways to try to control a situation or a person that has failed to meet our expectations.

Inward directed aggression. Suicide is the most destructive of the inwardly directed violence; it is a way to take control by removing ourselves from the painful situation. Two of the groups most susceptible to this inner aggression are the young and the elderly. For both, the future seems out of their control and the present is confusing and painful. Suicide offers the only way out of their pain without "hurting anyone," Guilt, low self-esteem, and many other factors play important roles in this destructive and sad behavior. Self-destruction can take other expressions such as addiction to drugs, alcohol, food, sex, work, gambling, depression, and so on. The pattern is the same even when the actions differ. It is our way of saying, "Stop the world, I want to get out!"

More common forms of inwardly passive aggression are illnesses that do not have an apparent physical cause. Headaches, stomach disorders, ulcers, and many other symptoms reflect a deeper reality: something is upsetting us. Hopefully, we are willing to choose to look at anger face to face and allow it to talk to us. What will we hear when we listen to this powerful emotion?

First of all, we will discover that the emotion itself is friendly; it is actually "on our side," trying to tell us that something is not right in our lives. As we have seen, anger begins as a response to a perceived hurt or injustice in a situation that is not the way we think it should be or a person who does not treat us the way we would like. Thus, anger begins with us; we are the authors of our own anger. No one has the power to make us feel angry; we must own it! In this sense, anger, just like pain, is my friend, a companion in my journey calling me to growth and health.

Once we are open to hearing the voice of God in our anger, we need to pay attention to God's message. God might be asking me to lower my expectations, to remember that my family and friends are not gods and cannot give me what I need or want. God could be asking me to spend less energy complaining about the limitations of those around me and invest more in working on my own.

Sometimes the situation calls for a change. My anger may be justified because my husband is physically or mentally abusing me and our children. After trying every possible solution, the only thing left is to end the relationship. This decision requires a lot of prayer, discernment, and possibly counseling, and cannot be taken lightly. When we end a relationship with a person or with a community, forgiveness plays an important role in the process. Without forgiveness, the anger will continue to poison us even if we leave the situation.

God could also be calling me to take a prophetic stance before an injustice. Every time God called a prophet to speak in God's name, the emotions of love, anger, and compassion were present. We need to listen to our anger before it leads us to violence, just as we need to listen to our pain before it turns into suffering.

It may sound crazy, but I believe that without the energies of love, pain, anger, and many others, creation would be less than it is meant to be. Growth and development involve change, and change is always painful and frustrating. It would be of great benefit for the entire Body if we decided to put our energies, whatever they may be, into positive actions that could lead to healing, rather than wasting them in hatred, anger, and revenge.

Chapter 5

The Mystery of Suffering

The man who has not suffered,
what can he possibly know, anyway?
—Rabbi Abraham Joshua Heschel

I begin this chapter on suffering reminding myself that I am still navigating in an ocean of mystery. A mystery is by definition unknowable. The mysteries of God, evil, and suffering will continue to fascinate us, precisely because we cannot make sense of them. That does not mean that we must ignore them or push them aside. They are and will always be faithful companions in our journey. True, we will never understand them, but hopefully we can reach a place where we feel comfortable with what our faith and life experiences reveal to us about these mysteries.

Pain and Suffering

Pain is an intrinsic part of living. To live is to be constantly changing, and change is always painful. The only people who feel no pain "live" in cemeteries! Pain may be qualified as follows:

- Physical: illnesses, accidents, diminishments of old age, anything that impinges on our sense of well-being.
- Psychological: Maybe I do not have a biological problem with my heart; nonetheless, my heart aches because of a broken relationship or the loss of a loved one.
- Spiritual pain: Ignatius of Loyola called it desolation; John of the Cross coined the term "the dark night." I frequently use the phrase "spiritual dehydration" to describe some of the symptoms of spiritual pain.

Regardless of the kind of pain, no one wants it. Why did I get this illness? Why am I losing my spouse now when we are just beginning our lives together? Why can't I pray when God knows how much I need to be comforted? Why can't I feel his presence with me? Why me?

We all share pain because we live in an imperfect world where "IT" happens. Pain reminds us that we are evolving, growing, and not yet in paradise. As St. Irenaeus and Teilhard believed, we and creation are in the process of development, and pain is part of this evolution. Yet pain does not need to become suffering.

I once read in a book on Eastern spirituality that pain is part of living, but suffering is optional. Obviously, this is an issue of semantics, and it all depends on the meaning we ascribe to each word, but the statement had an impact on me then and still does today. Using these words in a new context might bring new insights, not as an attempt to undermine suffering or its religious connotation, but by offering a different way of viewing pain that may help us handle it better.

Even those who believe that suffering is important for their spiritual growth do not really enjoy it. If we are going to "suffer," let it be for a good reason and not simply because we do not know how to manage pain.

People's attitudes toward pain take into account whether the pain is useful or useless, deserved or undeserved. Usually we handle better a pain that we caused than a pain that literally "came from nowhere." Let us take for example exercising. It might leave us exhausted, but it is useful: good for our health, weight, looks, and so on. If I insist on climbing to the top of the Empire State Building knowing that I am afraid of heights, I am certainly looking for psychological pain. If after the experience I complain, someone will remind me that I did it to myself.

Most of us are aware that pain simply "happens," with or without our intervention, and we accept that as part of life. "Suffering," on the other hand, is very subjective. Two people are involved in a minor car accident, and they both break an arm. They undoubtedly are in pain, but the degree of suffering is relative. One takes it with a grain of salt as part of living, while the other wastes energies asking, "Why me? Why now?" What makes one person suffer deeply may leave another untouched. Our response to what happens is more important than the actual event. One person's experience drives him or her to curse God, while another's identical experience drives him or her to bless God.

Moreover, some things that we consider tragic may appear so only because of the obvious limitations in our cultural contexts and individual perspectives. For example, if I overvalue productivity, then getting older or sick would be tragic; if I place my worth on material possessions, any loss of income will cause much pain; if I use relationships solely for self-gratification, anyone who ignores me or refuses to fulfill my desires will become a thorn in my side. More often than not, when viewed from a distance and through the eyes of faith, things that appear to be painful ultimately bring about a greater good.

Pain and suffering are mysteries, and one event may be good or bad depending on how we look at it and process it.

A friend of mine is a nurse. A few years ago her father had a heart attack while they were having lunch. She applied CPR and called the paramedics, who took him to the nearest hospital. Her father survived and had a total recovery. Everyone praised my friend for "saving" the man, who was only in his early fifties. She was proud and grateful for this opportunity our good God had given her. Less than a year later, her father began to complain about severe headaches. The diagnosis was an inoperable malignant brain tumor! He died after a few months of terrible suffering. His was one of the most horrible deaths I have ever witnessed.

My friend felt guilty. Her father could have had a peaceful death the year before, but because of her intervention he had suffered hell on earth. Whom to blame? Herself for interfering with life's process? God for not stopping her attempts to save him? God and suffering appeared to be so interconnected that no one knew what to say. One day as we were sharing about her pain, she became aware that the last time that she had seen her father on his deathbed, she had felt the presence of God in him, his distorted face reminded her of Jesus on the cross. I affirmed the experience, and her sorrow began to be transformed into hope. Because of this entire process, my friend has become a wiser and more compassionate person. She now knows that we do not have an answer for the mystery of life and death, but she is moving on with her life, developing as a true human being in union with the One who loves her. She still has moments of pain and grief, but never frustration or suffering.

South Florida is the land of sunshine and hurricanes. During hurricane season (June–November), everyone is on standby. We have to be prepared, get the shutters ready, buy enough water and food to last for at least three weeks, plan where to go if we need to evacuate, and then wait! For some people, this waiting is a period of suffering. They believe every prediction they hear and are anticipating the loss of everything they own. Hurricanes often change their course at the last minute, so we need to be prepared for the season but not panic until the storm is twenty-four to forty-eight hours away.

Others are relaxed because they have lived through many storms and trust that sooner or later everything will go back to normal. They prepare their home, cars, and other possessions, and then leave the rest to God. I don't know how much faith they have, but at least they are smart enough to realize that worrying will not help the crisis except by making the whole family hysterical. Same stimulus, two different reactions. A large part of our "suffering" could be avoided with the right attitude.

In every situation, dealing with pain or any strong emotion, our response will depend on how we use its energy: to get better, to engage in healing practices, to speak to wisdom people. Or perhaps we choose to waste it complaining about our bad luck, or blaming others for our misery.

Do you have any idea how much energy it takes to be angry, to hold grudges, to plan revenge, or to look for someone to blame for your pain? Whatever we do with that energy is up to us. Actually, the question of why bad things happen to good people should be, "What do good people intend to do with what happens to them?"

I am scheduled to have a total knee replacement in exactly two months. In the meantime, I get shots of steroids in my knee every six weeks. Because of other physical conditions, I need two months for preliminary tests to guarantee the safety of the surgery. Three weeks ago I had a shot and, as usual, it made the pain bearable but only for a few days. For the first time, the pain started again with a vengeance four days later, making it very hard for me to walk. For the last week I have been sitting in my recliner, with my leg up, and my tiny notebook on my lap. I was frustrated and confused about this new development. I felt helpless; I was suffering! Yesterday, I reviewed what I had been writing in the book and decided to "snap out of it." My hypothesis about pain and suffering was not working for me! I had to do something.

Many years ago when I was in my early twenties, I went through a period of questioning. I questioned the existence of God, the issues of evil and suffering, the death of my father, my illnesses, and many other things. At the time I had a spiritual director, a wise older Jesuit, who knew me inside out. In one of the sessions during a weekend retreat, I began with my litany of questions. He instructed me to go pray and not to come back until I had an answer for at least one of them.

The following day I returned frustrated and angry with him. I said, "You don't understand the depth of my questions. They are foundational to my faith, I cannot find any answers. I think I am losing my faith!" He gave me one of his "killer smiles" and asked, "How long are you going to be a teenager? These are the same questions I get from my students at the high school. When are you going to grow up?" I was furious and humiliated, so I asked (rather loudly), "What do you want me to do? What is your wise solution?" He looked at me the way Jesus must have looked at the rich young man, and said, "Act as if you believed!" I did, and my doubts stopped and never came back.

Yesterday I decided to follow his advice as I have done many times before in different contexts. I informed my family that today I would be well. Of course, I got "the looks." I told them that I refused to continue suffering like this and feeling helpless. "Tomorrow I will act *as if* I am better," I said. Last night, my prayer went something like this: "God, you know what I have decided to do. I only see three possible scenarios: (1) Things will continue the same, the pain will not increase, and I will simply move on. (2) Moving around and walking may cause whatever is out of whack to come back to its place, and I will feel better until my next shot and the surgery. (3) The knee will snap, the pain will become intolerable, and I will have to be rushed to the hospital. God, I don't know what will happen, but this is all I am able to do. I will act *as if* I am better and you do the rest. Any of the three scenarios are acceptable to me."

This morning I took a shower, prayed, put on my knee brace and started to insert this story in the appropriate place. Later, I might go to the supermarket to get a few things we need. "Brother pain" is with me, but I am not suffering!

God Suffers with Us

> Some things about God are becoming clearer. For example, with regard to the great problem of suffering in the world, we have moved from seeing God as the cause of this suffering, to seeing God as the one who allows people to suffer, to seeing God as the one who is suffering with us. God is to be found among the victims of injustice, those who are sinned against, the poor and the marginalized, the sick and the outcasts.[1]

This position is hard to accept especially in religious circles. For most Christians, God is never "messy," but I am absolutely convinced that God feels my pain with me.

When I was around thirty years old, I was diagnosed with rheumatoid arthritis (R.A.). At the time, the only effective treatment to control the pain and allow me to walk was heavy doses of steroids. My doctor warned me that the amount of Prednisone that I was taking was going to limit my life span and cause other serious problems. Of course, I did not have much choice; it was either a long, crippled life or a shorter one with more quality. I chose the quality. My family and friends showed compassion, or maybe pity, and some asked how God could allow this to happen to such a good person.

I must admit that I never considered that question. I believed in the goodness of God and in the fact that "IT" happens! To me, God is neither the author of evil nor its helpless victim. Rather, precisely because of God's awesome love, goodness, and respect for me, I intuited that God had chosen to coexist with my "mess" to see me through and to bring light into my darkness. My job was to become a "seer" and to find God in the midst of "IT."

My R.A. and other illnesses that followed have helped me appreciate living in the now, in the present moment. I also enjoy more the beauty of nature and the outdoors. Seeing the children growing up is terrific, and since I cannot play rough with them, I use my gift of photography to capture their beautiful faces, their funny gestures, and their budding idiosyncrasies.

I love cruising and never cease to be amazed at the grandeur of our universe. I continue to sail to different places on this wonderful planet, but I stay on the ship and look out to the sea and the sky, the sun and the moon; they all remind me of how blessed I am to be able to see all this beauty.

Today is all I have, and I try to make the most out of it. Am I in pain? For sure. Am I suffering? Definitely not! I will not give the pain the power to stop me from enjoying life. I believe that physical limitations have made me a better person. I seldom worry about the future, because I have lived many "futures" when they were "presents," and God was always there. Contemplative prayer comes easily for me because my physical limitations make me less active now, and for this I am very grateful.

I feel deep compassion for people in pain, and I find it easy to listen for as long as it takes. I have been a spiritual companion for people who are dying of cancer and for others who have lost a loved one. I am not afraid of pain or of death, so I can walk the walk when needed. I owe all these gifts to my illnesses.

In the past two years, I have had several surgeries and stayed in the hospital many times. "IT" happens, but it is so wonderful and comforting to know that I do not need to "look" for God anywhere or to "ask" God to help me. God simply is in "IT" with me and I know that God feels the same fears and anxiety that I feel. I once read the story of a peasant in the early 1900s who, upon leaving his home, always said, "Good bye, Lord God, I am going to church to perform my religious duties." So true! We keep on looking for God in designated "holy or sacred places" and forget that the entire universe is sacred and that special wonders like the Grand Canyon are really God's cathedrals.

Moreover, because I believe that the world is in the process of becoming, as are all the creatures, suffering is "the natural spin-off, the inevitable growing pains of matter and spirit evolving from fetal immaturity to fullness of being" (see Romans 8:22-23).[2]

It is in moments like this that I go through the exercise of welcoming the pain. As long as I see pain as an enemy, it will hurt. Once I accept my pain as a companion in my journey of faith, the suffering is gone even if the pain remains. Pain does not take away my spiritual energies the way suffering does. When we speak of suffering in religious circles, there is no distinction between pain and suffering. Suffering is the traditional word used in the Bible to describe both. When the saints wrote on suffering, they did not have in mind any distinctions and even less the possibility to "embrace pain in order to avoid suffering." Thomas Merton was able to combine the two concepts when he wrote, "The truth that many people never understand, until it is too late, is that the more you try to avoid suffering the more you suffer because smaller and more insignificant things begin to torture you in proportion to your fear of being hurt."[3]

Francis of Assisi and Suffering

Francis of Assisi saw in every creature a brother or a sister. That included sister illness, brother sun, brother fire, sister water, and ultimately sister death. Francis suffered physical, emotional, and spiritual pain, but he was always joyful, because he used the energies of his pain to love God and all God's creatures.

Few people know that when Francis wrote his famous "Canticle to the Creatures," he was blind, in terrible pain, and dying. Actually he dictated it to one of his brothers. His energies went to praise creation not to control him with self-pity or overwhelming suffering.

Francis is known for his joyful disposition and his celebration of the goodness of God and the beauty of creation. Many spiritual writers attribute these qualities to his progress in the way of detachment, the art of letting go. I would like to suggest another possibility, simply because the word "detachment" still holds a negative connotation. If Francis of Assisi found God in everything and everything in God, including illness, rejection, and pain, why would he choose to "detach" from any part of God's creation?

Webster defines detachment as "separate; not connected; disinterested." There is something inhuman about this definition. For a believer, these words convey a lack of interest in the process of creation, giving up "worldly values for the sake of spiritual things" (there is that dualism again!). Some people want to look so holy by pretending to be indifferent to their pain that they become bitter and proud. If the acceptance of "brother pain" is not real, it will eventually show in negative and harmful ways toward others.

This is not what Francis did. I believe the confusion comes from the traditional understanding of a detachment that urges us to let go of things *not in God*. But is there anything that *is not in God?* Is it not the biblical understanding that there is no place where I can run from God's love, because in God I live and move and have my being and that no one or no thing can take me away from the love of God in Christ Jesus? (see Psalm 139; Acts 17:28; Romans 8:39).

It is said that Teresa of Avila was so taken with her Beloved that she completely forgot herself. Her poetry confirms this. Teresa's experience speaks to me of love not of separation and estrangement. Recently I read that detachment is really "non-attachment: the readiness to forego [*sic*] a good thing for a better, yet never denying its goodness."[4]

Francis of Assisi lived attached to God and to the evangelical life in the spirit of freedom and availability to God. For him as well as for Teresa, detachment was the realization that, when one is with God, nothing else is needed. God suffices. Perhaps one of the most popular aspects of Franciscan spirituality is the unity that Francis saw in all creation. He lived in union with God, who is present in all things. For him, creation was not a distraction or an obstacle to his union with God; he reveled in the glory of God in creation. In his "Testament," he writes,

> This is how God inspired me, Brother Francis, to embark upon a life of penance (conversion). When I was in sin, the sight of lepers nauseated me beyond measure; but then God Himself led me into their company, and I had pity on them. When I had once become acquainted with them, what had previously nauseated me became a source of spiritual and physical consolation for me.[5]

Francis was comfortable with his feelings and actually used his senses to discern God's presence. Nausea, consolation, and sweetness were ways in which God spoke to him. Francis was able to find God in everyday life, quick to see that every small part of God's universe was a gift that his Beloved was offering him.

Francis also had a deep love for Lady Poverty. He instructed his followers to appropriate nothing for themselves, "neither a house, nor a place, nor anything else . . . they should beg alms trustingly. And there is no reason why they should be ashamed, because God made himself poor for us in this world."[6] Without a doubt, Christ was for Francis the icon of the Creator.

Francis desired to follow the poor Christ, and, for a joyful extrovert such as he was, that meant living at the margins of the society of his time with the lepers, the poor, and those considered of little worth. Poverty for Francis was not a form of asceticism or self-denial; he actually felt called to follow the poor Christ in the poor. For Francis, detachment was an "invitation to share the creative inner liberty of Christ himself. Christ was truly a free man."[7] "Jesus was stupefyingly free. He was able to stand up and contradict the assumptions, customs, and cultural norms of his society. . . . He was free to love without reserve, to love the poorest of the poor as well as the rich young man. The pious would have been scandalized by the love and concern he showed for prostitutes."[8]

As I mentioned before in the chapter on evil, freedom is a gift from the Creator that cannot be endangered by idolatry. Just as an exaggerated desire for power, relationships, or money can lead us to idolatry, an exaggerated need for "happiness" and well-being can lead us to suffering.

Francis was a happy saint.

> If a saint's version of happiness meant being eaten by lions or wearing a hair shirt, it would likely attract few takers. But it is a mistake to identify saints with hardship and misery. In general they were renowned for their balance and good humor, their compassion and generosity, their spirit of peace and freedom in the face of obstacles and adversities, and their ability to find joy in all things.[9]

Although most people do not use my distinction between pain and suffering, I have found several writings on the lives of the saints that point out that pain or suffering is not the opposite of happiness. Francis of Assisi coined the concept of "perfect joy," which had to do not with happiness, but with the inner peace that Christ gave us after the resurrection.

One winter day St. Francis was coming to St. Mary of the Angels from Perugia with Brother Leo, and the bitter cold made them suffer keenly. St. Francis called to Brother Leo, and he said: "Brother Leo, even if a Friar Minor gives sight to the blind, heals the paralyzed, drives out devils, gives hearing back to the deaf, makes the lame walk, and restores speech to the dumb, and what is still more, brings back to life a man who has been dead four days, write that perfect joy is not in that." . . . And going on a bit farther, St. Francis called again strongly: "Brother Leo, even if a Friar Minor could preach so well that he should convert all infidels to the faith of Christ, write that perfect joy is not there." Now when he had been talking this way for a distance of two miles, Brother Leo in great amazement asked him: "Father, I beg you in God's name to tell me where perfect joy is." And St. Francis replied; "When we come to St. Mary of the Angels, soaked by the rain and frozen by the cold, all soiled with mud and suffering from hunger, and we ring at the gate of the Place and the brother porter comes and says angrily: 'Who are you?' And we say: 'We are two of your brothers.' And he contradicts us, saying: 'You are not telling the truth. Rather you are two rascals who go around deceiving people and stealing' . . . and he does not open for us, but makes us stand outside in the snow and rain, cold and hungry . . . if we endure all those insults and cruel rebuffs patiently, without being troubled and without complaining. . . . Oh, Brother Leo, write that perfect joy is there! . . . And now hear the conclusion,

> Brother Leo. Above all the graces and gifts of the Holy Spirit which Christ gives to His friends is that of conquering oneself and willingly enduring sufferings, insults, humiliations, and hardships for the love of Christ."[10]

For Francis, imitating the suffering Christ was "perfect joy." This is a way that many Christians have followed. The important detail to remember is that the only way to welcome "brother suffering" is with joy. Suffering can make us bitter and close us down, or it can make us wise, compassionate, and utterly open to God and the suffering of others.

Jesus, Evil, and Suffering in the New Testament

The notion that God wishes suffering upon the world is heretical. Yet I know some people who think that way. They imagine God sitting on his high throne distributing talents, beauty, deformities, mental and physical challenges, intelligence, and so on, to the babies waiting in line to receive them. As a matter of fact, we often say about a bright person, "Wow, when God was distributing intelligence, you must have been the first one in the line." I am aware that these remarks are not to be taken literally, but unfortunately the covert message they carry is there and it gets through.

I have heard comments like this about a severely handicapped boy: "He is all goodness and love. God made him that way, and God does not make junk." I have also heard the opposite when talking to a mother about her gorgeous little girl: "You must feel very grateful to God for blessing you with such a beautiful child!" These actually are love comments, but if I am the mother of the mentally challenged boy, how can I thank God for that blessing when I have in front of me the happy mother of the brilliant kid?

Jesus came to reveal to us a loving God. If we believe this, then we must pay attention to what Jesus said and did in his time about suffering.

- He never taught that pain was good in itself. He healed the sick in body and mind, continuing the work of his Father:

  > *The man went away and told the Jews that it was Jesus who had made him well. Therefore the Jews started persecuting Jesus, because he was doing such things [healing] on the Sabbath. But Jesus answered them,* "My Father is still working, and I also am working."
  >
  > —John 5:15-17

- Jesus devoted his life to reducing human suffering, and the Sabbath law or the scorn of the Jewish religious leaders did not stop him:

  > *He was teaching in one of the synagogues on the sabbath. And just then there appeared a woman with a spirit that had crippled her for eighteen years. She was bent over. . . . When Jesus saw her, he called her over and said, "Woman, you are set free from your ailment." . . . But the leader of the synagogue, indignant because Jesus had cured on the sabbath, kept saying to the crowd, "There are six days on which work ought to be done; come on those days and be cured,*

> *and not on the sabbath day." But the Lord answered him and said, "You hypocrites! Does not each of you on the sabbath untie his ox or his donkey from the manger, and lead it away to give it water? And ought not this woman, a daughter of Abraham whom Satan bound for eighteen long years, be set free from this bondage on the sabbath day?"*
>
> —Luke 13:10-16

- Satan could not defeat Jesus when he tempted him in the desert: "Then the devil left him, and suddenly angels came and waited on him" (Matthew 4:1-11)
- Jesus rejected the notion that sickness is the result or punishment for a person's sins or for the sins of his or her ancestors:

> *As he walked along, he saw a man blind from birth. His disciples asked him, "Rabbi, who sinned, this man or his parents, that he was born blind?" Jesus answered, "Neither this man nor his parents sinned; he was born blind so that God's works might be revealed in him. We must work the works of him who sent me while it is day; night is coming when no one can work. As long as I am in the world, I am the light of the world."*
>
> —John 9:1-5

Jesus was ridiculed and laughed at by many who did not believe in his power to heal or to bring a little girl back from the dead. His desire to heal and to help people live their lives to the fullest was stronger than the mockery and insults he experienced:

> *When he had entered, he said to them, "Why do you make a commotion and weep? The child is not dead but sleeping." And they laughed at him. Then he put them all outside, and took the child's father and mother and those who were with him, and went in where the child was. He took her by the hand and said to her, "Talitha cum," which means, "Little girl, get up!" And immediately the girl got up and began to walk about (she was twelve years of age). At this they were overcome with amazement.*
> —Mark 5:39-42

- God loves us with an unconditional love, wants us to be happy, and desires to comfort us. But it is up to us, co-creators, to make it happen. So Jesus challenged his disciples to care for the suffering of the world:

  > *Come, you that are blessed by my Father, inherit the kingdom prepared for you from the foundation of the world; for I was hungry and you gave me food. . . . Then the righteous will answer him, "Lord, when was it that we saw you hungry and gave you food? . . ." And the king will answer them, "Truly I tell you, just as you did it to one of the least of these who are members of my family, you did it to me."*
  > —Matthew 25:37-40

- Even the most powerful evil could not stop Jesus. But, when the townspeople who had lived with a possessed man for years witnessed the man's deliverance, they became afraid of Jesus, the one who had freed him. Often we are afraid of the freedom that God wants to give us and prefer to continue living in the slavery that is familiar to us:

> *When he had stepped out of the boat, immediately a man out of the tombs with an unclean spirit met him . . . no one could restrain him any more, even with a chain. . . . When he saw Jesus from a distance, he ran and bowed down before him; and he shouted at the top of his voice, "What have you to do with me, Jesus, Son of the Most High God? I adjure you by God, do not torment me." For he had said to him, "Come out of the man, you unclean spirit!" Then Jesus asked him, "What is your name?" He replied, "My name is Legion; for we are many." And the unclean spirits came out. . . . Then people came to see what it was that had happened. They came to Jesus and saw the demoniac sitting there, clothed and in his right mind, the very man who had had the legion; and they were afraid. . . . Then they began to beg Jesus to leave their neighborhood.*
> —Mark 5:2-3, 6-9, 13-17

Jesus is the icon of God. He said, "Whoever sees me, sees the Father." The feelings that Jesus expresses in his humanity are the feelings of God; his pain is God's pain; his suffering is God's suffering. On the other hand, his desire to heal everyone is also God's desire; his victory over evil is God's victory; his outrageous love for sinners and outcasts is also a reflection of God's compassionate love toward all. When Jesus says that he is the Good Shepherd who has come so that we may have life, he means the perfect life of God in which we share—God's freedom and capacity to love and to create.

Earlier, when I shared the story of my little cousin dying of leukemia, I wrote the subheading "God the Thief." When her mother's friends told her that God had taken her daughter to be a little angel in heaven, they were describing the thief that comes to steal, kill, and destroy. What a miserable image of God to offer to a grieving mother!

> *So again Jesus said to them, "Very truly, I tell you . . . The thief comes only to steal and kill and destroy. I came that they may have life, and have it abundantly. I am the good shepherd. The good shepherd lays down his life for the sheep. The hired hand, who is not the shepherd and does not own the sheep, sees the wolf coming and leaves the sheep and runs away—and the wolf snatches them and scatters them.*
>
> —John 10:7-14

> *And as he sat at dinner in Levi's house, many tax collectors and sinners were also sitting with Jesus and his disciples. . . . When the scribes of the Pharisees saw that he was eating with sinners and tax -collectors, they said to his disciples, "Why does he eat with tax -collectors and sinners?" When Jesus heard this, he said to them, "Those who are well have no need of a physician, but those who are sick; I have come to call not the righteous but sinners."*
>
> —Mark 2:15-17

Jesus dedicated his life and ministry to alleviating suffering and showing a new way of living. To those who may lose hope because of personal and communal suffering in our world I say, "IT" happens, but the good news is that God is not the *cause*, nor did God *allow* it, but God is right in the middle of "IT," sharing our mess, comforting us and bringing light into the darkness. God shares in our suffering and calls for a similar attitude from us. As God comforts us, so we are to comfort others.

> *Blessed be the God and Father of our Lord Jesus Christ, the Father of mercies and the God of all consolation, who consoles us in all our affliction, so that we may be able to console those who are in any affliction with the consolation with which we ourselves are consoled by God. . . . Our hope for you is unshaken; for we know that as you share in our sufferings, so also you share in our consolation.*
>
> —2 Corinthians 1:3-4, 7

Redemptive Suffering

> *I am now rejoicing in my sufferings for your sake, and in my flesh I am completing what is lacking in Christ's afflictions for the sake of his body, that is, the church.*
>
> —Colossians 1:24

This text from St. Paul has always bothered me. I waited until the chapter was almost finished to deal with the topic of redemptive suffering, and honestly, the reason is my own discomfort with the traditional understanding of this concept.

Paul's words seem to imply that Jesus' suffering was incomplete or insufficient and that our sufferings are also needed somehow to finish God's plan for the world. I find this concept hard to accept. First, I cannot believe in a God who needs someone to suffer and die to placate his wrath. Worse than that is the Jewish notion that there was an allotted amount of suffering that had to be completed before God was satisfied. These concepts are so totally contrary to my image and experience of God that I try to ignore them even when they are included in so many of our liturgical prayers.

I read somewhere that if the Creator of the sun, the moon, and the stars was crowned with thorns on his head, beaten, and nailed to a cross, why should we be spared? This sounds very pious and holy, but I did not create anything, so why should I suffer because God decided to make himself a world? If indeed Christ has already "paid" the debt, why do I need to keep on paying?

In my opinion, these are misinterpretations of key passages from the Bible, which, taken literally, seem to support these ideas. For centuries, flawed catechesis has presented God in the business of selling "salvation," "indulgences," and the like, to those who fulfill certain requirements. If one fails to pray novenas, attend Mass on the First Fridays, or pray the Divine Mercy Chaplets, one will have a tough time getting close to God. This teaching has controlled many people for centuries and kept them fearing God.

In addition, I believe that the concept of suffering has been overplayed. I feel very uncomfortable when people who are familiar with my illnesses tell me that I am blessed and that God must love me very much to let me share in the sufferings of his Son. I usually do not know what to say, and I look for an excuse to leave. I do not consider myself blessed by illnesses or chosen by God to share the pain of his Son. I am so turned off by these teachings that I decided to offer an alternative explanation of "redemptive suffering" that makes sense to me. I was once told that one should never take something away from a person if one cannot replace it with something else. I want to offer other ways of interpreting redemptive suffering, hoping that it will help those who might feel as frustrated as I do with the current teachings.

Redemptive Suffering (my version)

- I believe that the risen, Cosmic Christ is alive in every member of his Mystical Body. In the First Letter to the Corinthians Paul tells us, "If one member suffers, all suffer together with it; if one member is honored, all rejoice together with it . . . [we] are the body of Christ and individually members of it" (1 Corinthians 12:26-27). The way I interpret this text is that, because of the unity of the members among themselves and with Christ, the ongoing sufferings of the risen Christ, who is very much alive in his Body, and my sufferings are united. To paraphrase Matthew 25, whatever I do with my sufferings (positive or negative) I do it to Christ and therefore to the Body. As a Body, we cooperate with God in profound and mysterious ways that benefit one another. This makes sense to me.

  I found the same concept affirmed by William J. O'Malley:

> The "sufferings of Christ" has two senses: the sufferings of the historical God-Man on Calvary, and the suffering of the new Body of Christ: the Church. Thus, Christ—in his extension in the Church—must go on suffering. Each of us must play his or her part in bearing our common burden. . . . The sufferings of the Christ did not cease when Jesus died. Christ still suffers, when we suffer, and—we trust—our suffering is redemptive just as his sufferings were redemptive.[11]

- If we believe, as I do, that in Christ, God suffers with me, it makes sense to say that we both share in the same sufferings. If God is willing to take on my sufferings, I am willing to take on someone else's suffering for the love of God. In Christ, God suffered rejection, betrayal, misunderstanding, physical and emotional pain; I am willing to do the same for my brothers and sisters in their need. Moreover, I know that I have to do it graciously and without bitter complaining so as not to affect negatively the well-being of the Body.
- I am always grateful and moved by someone who suffers an inconvenience for my sake (for example, taking me to the hospital at 5:00 A.M., helping me get clean when I am incapacitated, etc.). I am touched when I think of what my mother went through when she sent my brother and me to the United States or when one of the Sisters donated her blood for my surgery. There is "no greater love." I do believe that their suffering is

redemptive. I believe we are all called to this kind of suffering, to lay down our lives for our friends.

- When St. Maximilian Kolbe gave his life in Auschwitz to save a young man, that was redemptive suffering. His act of selflessness and unconditional love for a total stranger made his suffering part of creation's growing pains, redemptive suffering!
- Richard Rohr observes:

> Things happen *against your will*—which is what makes it suffering . . . you have no choice. *The situation is what it is*. The suffering might feel wrong, terminal, absurd, unjust, impossible, physically painful, or just outside of your comfort zone. . . . We must have a proper attitude toward suffering, because many things every day leave us out of control. . . . Remember always, however, that *if you do not transform your pain, you will surely transmit it to those around you and even to the next generation.*[12]

This will be negative energy that will affect the Body of Christ.

These words of wisdom about how to deal with suffering not only help me grow and become a better person but also benefit those around me.

> God, grant me the serenity to accept the things
> I cannot change; courage to change the things I can;
> and wisdom to know the difference.
>
> —Reinhold Niebuhr[13]

- Teilhard de Chardin explains magnificently and creatively the concept of redemptive suffering:

  > What a vast ocean of human suffering spreads over the entire earth at every moment! Of what is this mass formed? . . . Let me repeat, of *potential energy*. In suffering, the ascending force of the world is concealed in a very intense form. The whole question is how to liberate it and give it a consciousness of its significance and potentialities. The world would leap high toward God if all the sick together were to turn their pain into a common desire that the kingdom of God should come to rapid fruition through the conquest and organization of the earth.
  >
  > All the sufferers of the earth joining their sufferings so that the world's pain might become a great and unique act of consciousness, elevation, and union. Would not this be one of the highest forms that the mysterious work of creation could take in our sight?[14]

- I feel energized by the idea that, as a member of the Body of Christ, my sufferings are helping to build up the Body. In addition, if Christ is the one who holds creation together, then it makes sense to say that my sufferings are also contributing to the evolution of the human consciousness and the consciousness of all creation. I must say that this approach is the most sensible and appealing that I am aware of.

- Suffering has opened for me the doors to a stronger faith and a deeper trust in God. If I had been a super-healthy person, I probably would have relied much less on God. I once found a message in my voice mail from a friend after one of my surgeries. All the others were wishing me a speedy recovery and lamenting my suffering. The message of this wisdom lady (now with God) went something like this: "Welcome home, my dear Adele. I just wanted to tell you that I give thanks to God every day for all your illnesses. If you had been healthy, it would have been very difficult to deal with you. Your illnesses are making you such a good person! God is good and is blessing you!" What can I say? She was right!
- Franciscan Friar Richard Rohr draws a masterful parallel between love and suffering. According to Rohr, until we love and suffer, we attempt to understand life and all its mysteries with our minds. But once we know the love that is beyond all knowledge (Ephesians 3:19) we are changed.

  > Love, I believe, is the only way to initially and safely open the door of awareness and aliveness, and the suffering for that love keeps that door open and available for ever greater growth. They are the two great doors, and we dare not leave them closed. . . . There is a straight line between love and suffering. If you love greatly, it is fairly certain you will soon suffer, because you have somehow given up control to another."[15]

Death and Eternal Life:
The Final YES and the Ultimate Mysteries

> Perhaps they are not stars, but rather openings in heaven where the love of our lost ones pours through and shines down upon us to let us know they are happy.
>
> —Eskimo Proverb

Death is the final question wrapped in mystery about the meaning of life and the existence of God. Whether or not there is life after death and whether or not we believe in the resurrection, these are, without doubt, crucial topics for all human beings, especially those who profess to be Christians.

My mother suffered a lot during her life, especially the loss of my father at an early age. When she was dying of colon cancer at age seventy-five, I tried to lift up her spirits by reminding her that finally she was going to be with my father forever. She quickly said, "Well, it's all relative, because nobody including him ever came back to tell me if heaven really exists."

I could not believe my ears. I knew how much my mother had loved my father and how faithful she had been to his memory. How could she say something like that? I tried to talk her into some acceptance of a heaven where she would be with God, her husband, and the rest of her family and loved ones. She eventually became more open to this hope, but I think it was mostly to please me.

Sadly, my mother was not unique. In my personal life and ministry I have met hundreds of "active Catholics" who are afraid of dying and are not sure about an afterlife. This faith or lack of it determines how the actual moment of dying will be.

How do we reconcile these doubts with the centrality of the resurrection in our Christian faith? Every Sunday we confess, "We believe in the resurrection of the dead and life everlasting." Do we really mean it? When we look at the early Christian communities, we find that their faith was based on the resurrection of Jesus. The *kerygma*, or proclamation, was and is by definition a testimony to the resurrection. However, this central event of our faith cannot be proven historically or scientifically. History tells us that there was an empty tomb, but it cannot prove that Jesus rose from the dead.

Over two thousand years ago, three men were crucified in Roman-occupied Palestine. These executions were common at the time, used to punish criminals and anyone who threatened the Roman peace. These are the historical facts about the events on Mount Calvary. However, the followers of one of these convicts, convinced that he had risen, changed their lives radically. Those who had previously denied knowing Jesus began to proclaim his life, death, and resurrection. The cowards became martyrs, the timid leaders, and the sinners saints.

With faith in the resurrection, the first disciples began to understand the actions and the teachings of Jesus from a new perspective. Jesus had shown us the face of God: "Whoever has seen me has seen the Father " (John 14:9). The personal experience of the living Christ led the first men and women to become the foundation of the community of believers that today we call the Church.

The faith of this community was centered on the resurrection of Jesus and the unshakable certainty that his

Spirit lived within and among them. Eventually their faith led them to believe in the incarnation. John wrote in the years 90-95, "In the beginning was the Word . . . and the Word was God. . . . And the Word became flesh and lived among us" (John 1:1, 14). Jesus was the living Word of God, and he was no longer limited by time, space, or human flaws. Jesus had become the Christ, the Alpha and the Omega, the reason for creation and the thread that unites all beings, human or not. There was reason to celebrate; life made sense, and death did also.

Death and resurrection are mysteries. Paul wrote that the seed that is planted never looks like the tree that will spring from it. Similarly, the body that dies is not identical to the one that will be reborn (cf. 1 Corinthians 15:35-58).

I don't know what heaven will be like, and I cannot give evidence of the resurrection of Jesus. But I believe in the testimony of those who have preceded me, and, above all, I believe in my own experience of the living God. I believe in the communion of saints (canonized or not), and therefore I believe that life after death is also a communal life with God, with one another, and with the universe. I believe in a God who is love and who desires to be loved by us and would not allow death to be the end of this love story called creation. Without this faith, the life of the historical Jesus would be the life of just another interesting character in the history of humanity. The living Christ, the Omega Point, would be a fallacy, and I cannot accept this. I cannot because I feel the presence, the energy, the love, and the interconnectedness of all that is because of our convergence in Christ.

I thank God, because in the midst of the madness in which we live, I can look at this universe from the perspective of God and with a vision of eternity. And I have no doubt that in this heaven (wherever and whatever it will be) my parents' love pours through the stars and shines down on us to let us know they are happy.

Death is a different kind of phenomenon. People go on living a carefree life even if they question heaven. They are able to push eternal life aside or file it under "things to do someday" and move on. It is not the same with death. We worry about when and how we will die. How long do we have to live? Will our dying process be very painful?

Some theologians believe that death is the ultimate YES. This is a very insightful definition of death and also very connected with my previous comments on hell. If a person has been faithful to his or her relationship with God, has had moments of intimacy in prayer, has not fallen into the sin of idolatry, has loved friends and forgiven enemies, the final YES to God will be just a continuation of the "eternal life" that has already begun (cf. John 17:3).

On the other hand, people who have lived with their backs turned against God might not even recognize the presence of the divine when they see it.

When Blessed Mother Teresa was in Miami many years ago, a reporter asked her why she wasted her time with dying people instead of helping children who still had a chance at life. She answered that those homeless men and women dying on the streets of Calcutta had never known love. She wanted to show them a little love before they died, so that when the moment came for them to meet the real LOVE face to face, they could recognize it and say the ultimate YES.

I do not think that I could describe death any better. It is the final moment when all our "yeses" have a chance to become a Yes like the one Mary gave to the angel. With her Yes, Mary gave birth to the Word and began a pivotal moment in the process of creation: the incarnation. With our Yes, we will fully enter eternal life and then "we will see face to face . . . we will know fully, even as we have been fully known" (cf. 1 Corinthians 13:12).

Some ask, "If God is so forgiving and compassionate, why don't we wait until that final moment to give our yes?" There is logic in the question. Why live a good life when at the last minute we can have a conversion like that of the "good thief" and ask God to remember us? That will only take five minutes of good behavior in our lives. When I hear these arguments, I remember Mother Teresa's answer to the reporter, and I wish I could say to those people, "Yes, God is forgiving and merciful and promised paradise to the good thief at the last minute, but my question to you is: 'Can you be sure that after a lifetime of saying no over and over to God, you will recognize love when you see it? I personally, would not take that chance.'"

When I said earlier that God does not send anyone to hell, but rather people choose their own hell, this is exactly what I meant. After years of turning away from God and worshiping the idols of our culture, choosing "heaven" would not even be on the agenda of their final days.

Vatican II reminded us that

> it is in the face of death that the riddle of human existence grows most acute. Not only is man tormented by pain and by the advancing deterioration of his body, but even more so by a dread of perpetual extinction. . . . He rebels against death because he bears in himself an eternal seed which cannot

> be reduced to sheer matter. All the endeavors of technology, though useful in the extreme, cannot calm his anxiety; for prolongation of biological life is unable to satisfy that desire for higher life which is inescapably lodged in his breast.[16]

Why is it that we long to unveil the mystery and at the same time are afraid of it? We spend time and money attending spiritual retreats, reading spiritual books, going to church, and so on. But, when the final moment comes, we start questioning everything we said we believed during our life. Everyone knows a joke or a true story about someone calling the priest to visit a very sick person, only to have the person scream, "Not yet, not yet!"

There are also moments when we "see" God in the dying person.

My grandaunt died at age ninety-five. She was a holy woman, one of the most loving and generous persons I have ever known. She was also the youngest of nine children. For some reason, she was convinced that one of her missions in life, other than teaching, was to bury all the members of her family. Years went by and she lost her husband and all her sisters except my grandmother, with whom she lived. Two years before passing, my grandaunt fell and broke a hip. Given her age and general condition, the doctor said surgery was out of the question, and she probably would not live too long. For two years she was bedridden and totally disabled. Toward the end of this period, my grandmother took very ill and was rushed to the hospital, where she died after a couple of days. The family decided not to say anything to my grandaunt to spare her the pain of the loss of her last living sibling.

By this time she was almost unaware of her surroundings. She was almost blind and could hardly speak. A nurse was feeding her with a syringe filled with milk. On this particular day, my mother and my aunt were feeling extremely sad seeing her suffering. We started to pray together and suddenly we all realized that "Nena" would not die because in her mind she still had one sister to bury.

I asked everyone to please kneel around her bed and I held my grandaunt's hands in mine. I softly spoke to her and little by little she opened her eyes. I do not have the words to explain the shine and the beauty of those eyes and the love they were giving me. I said, "Nena, Grandma is gone. She got very sick and God took her. We buried her and she had a beautiful funeral. You do not have to worry about her any longer. You have been a wonderful woman all your life, always helping others and giving of yourself. God has a crown of roses waiting for you as a reward for all your goodness and because he loves you so much. You can go now into the Sacred Heart you always loved and who now is waiting for you with outstretched arms. I love you." She opened her shining eyes even more, gave me a beautiful smile and died.

I know she is in heaven with her entire family in the presence of God. Is this heaven another state of consciousness? A parallel universe? Another planet? I obviously do not know, but more important I don't care. I have lived with mystery all my life, and I know that a good God is behind all these veils. I know it, because I have experienced the width, the depth, and the height of God's love for us, no exceptions.

Thanks, Nena, for your many yeses and your final YES!

Chapter 6

Understanding Faith

To one who has faith, no explanation is necessary.
To one without faith, no explanation is possible.
—St. Thomas Aquinas

After writing these pages on God, evil, and suffering, I realize that in the end, it is all about faith!

I am satisfied with my work, I believe everything that I have written, and yet I cannot prove any of it. I do not have any concrete proof that the God I believe in is real; the way I see and handle evil offers no guarantees either, and my way of interpreting suffering is very subjective. I could say with my mother, "Nobody has come back to tell me there is a heaven!"

Ultimately, it is all mystery! Yet it is possible to delight in mystery; it is possible to have the assurance of things we have not seen but have felt and experienced. I agree with the words of Helen Keller, "Death is no more than passing from one room into another. But there's a difference for me, you know. Because in that other room I shall be able to see."[1] How did she know?

My experiences assure me that I will also be able to see. As I look back to some of my journals, I find words about the awesomeness of the Creator and of creation, words about pain and experiences of sin. They remind me of the reality of the things I cannot see and the wonder of all spiritual journeys in spite of the ups and downs, or maybe because of them.

> All I have seen teaches me to trust the Creator for all I have not seen.
>
> —Ralph Waldo Emerson[2]

These words explain my position better than I could. I think my faith has a lot to do with what I have already seen and experienced. If I am amazed at the little that I have seen, why not trust the Creator for what I have not seen?

I read some interesting concepts and obscure definitions about faith in the *Catholic Encyclopedia*. I did not find them helpful at all. According to the *Encyclopedia*, in the Old Testament, the word for faith means essentially "steadfastness, faithfulness," whether of God toward humans or of humans toward God.

In the New Testament, the meanings "to believe" and "belief" come to the fore; in Christ's speech, faith (Greek *pistis*) frequently means "trust" but also "belief." In Acts, the word is used objectively of the tenets of the Christians but is often to be rendered "belief." For some, faith is "trust and only trust."

I have participated in conversations about these different meanings, and, although they are interesting, I do not see how they help average Christians to get a better grasp of what their faith is all about.

The truth is that many theological writers of the present day are given to very loose thinking, and in nothing is this as evident as in their treatment of faith. In one article I read, "Trust in God is faith, faith is belief, belief may mean creed, but creed is not equivalent to trust in God." "How and by what influence," some ask "was the living faith transformed into the creed to be believed, the surrender to Christ into a philosophical Christology?"[3]

I must admit that I enjoyed this piece of research. In the first place, it affirmed my frequent use of the word "mystery." How can we talk about our faith if we cannot even agree on its definition? Second, I was able to see how confusing the term can be for the average person in the pew. Based on my experience, I echo the questions, "by what influence was the living faith transformed into a creed to be believed," or "the surrender to Christ into a philosophical Christology?"

It appears that if we want to talk about faith, we need to begin with the experience of God. This makes the conversation more difficult, since every experience is unique. Nevertheless, there are certain criteria to determine if our religious experiences are real or not. We need to evaluate the fruits of the experience and make sure that they benefit the person and the community. A true experience of God always makes the person more humble than before, aware and accepting of his or her talents and limitations and avoiding being self-centered. The outcome of the experience must be congruent with the life of the person. In addition, there is a growth in self-knowledge and a desire to continue this growth.

We must keep in mind these criteria before we make any decisions based on our religious experiences, no matter how real they appear to be.

Christian Doctrine

Christian doctrine generally maintains that God dwells in all Christians and that they can experience God directly through belief in Jesus. There are countless definitions of faith, but for the purposes of this chapter, I will use my interpretation of faith based on some New Testament narratives—what we could call "Faith 101."

- Mark 4:36-40:

  > *Leaving the crowd behind, they took him with them in the boat. . . . A great windstorm arose, and the waves beat into the boat, so that the boat was already being swamped. But he was in the stern, asleep on the cushion; and they woke him up and said to him, "Teacher, do you not care that we are perishing?" He woke up and rebuked the wind, and said to the sea, "Peace! Be still!" Then the wind ceased. . . . He said to them, "Why are you afraid? Have you still no faith?"*

  Jesus shows power over wind and sea. In the Christian community, this event was seen as a sign of Jesus' saving presence amid persecutions. It was meant to *strengthen their faith.*

- Mark 5:25-34:

  > *Now there was a woman who had been suffering from hemorrhages for twelve years.*

> *. . . [She] came up behind him [Jesus] in the crowd and touched his cloak, for she said, "If I but touch his clothes, I will be made well." Immediately her hemorrhage stopped. . . . He said to her, "Daughter, your faith has made you well; go in peace, and be healed of your disease."*

The woman was convinced *because of her faith* in Jesus that physical contact with his garment was enough to heal her.

- Matthew 9:2-6:

> *Some people were carrying a paralyzed man lying on a bed.* When Jesus saw their faith, *he said to the paralytic, "Take heart, son;* your sins are forgiven. . . . *so that you may know that the Son of Man has authority on earth to forgive sins"—he then said to the paralytic—"Stand up, take your bed and go to your home."*

It was the faith of the paralytic and his friends who carried him that moved Jesus to heal the man. Other miracles reveal Jesus' *emphasis on faith* as the requisite for healing.

- Matthew 9:27-30:

> *As Jesus went on from there, two blind men followed him, crying loudly, "Have mercy on us, Son of David!" . . . Jesus said to them, "Do you believe that I am able to do this?" They said to him, "Yes, Lord." Then he touched their eyes and said, "According to your faith let it be done to you." And their eyes were opened.*

These healings prepare the way for Jesus to answer to the emissaries of John the Baptist: "Go and tell John what you hear and see: the blind receive their sight, the lame walk, the lepers are cleansed" (Matthew 11:4-5).

- Luke 18:35-42:

  As he approached Jericho, a blind man was sitting by the roadside begging. . . . Then he shouted, "Jesus, Son of David, have mercy on me!" . . . [Jesus] asked him, "What do you want me to do for you?" He said, "Lord, let me see again." Jesus said to him, "Receive your sight; your faith has saved you."

  The blind man gives Jesus a title that is related to his role as Messiah. Through the "Son of David," healing comes to the blind man.

- Luke 17:5-6:

  The apostles said to the Lord, "Increase our faith!" The Lord replied, "If you had faith the size of a mustard seed, you could say to this mulberry tree, 'Be uprooted and planted in the sea,' and it would obey you."

  A mustard seed is very small. But once planted, it grows into a plant large enough to provide food and shelter for animals. Jesus said even a *little faith* can accomplish even impossible things.

- Luke 7:36-50:

  One of the Pharisees asked Jesus to eat with him. . . . And a woman in the city, who was a sinner . . . brought an alabaster jar of ointment. She stood behind him at his feet, weeping, and began to bathe his feet with

> *her tears and to dry them with her hair. Then she continued kissing his feet and anointing them with the ointment. . . . [Jesus said to Simon] "I tell you, her sins, which were many, have been forgiven; hence she has shown great love." . . . Then he said to her, "Your sins are forgiven. . . . Your faith has saved you; go in peace."*

> The sinful woman's faith in God led her to seek forgiveness for her sins, and because *so much was forgiven*, she now overwhelms Jesus with her love.

Healing in the New Testament is often connected to faith. The sick person asks for the miracle and believes that Jesus is capable of doing it. The Lord responds with the act of healing. We cannot guess the kind of faith to which the stories refer. Miracle healers were not uncommon in the area at the time, and people knew about them by word of mouth. We cannot assume that those who asked Jesus for a miracle at that time believed that he was the Son of God, or the Christ. These accounts were written after the resurrection from the perspective of the faith of the early Christian community. The strong belief in the resurrection colored the meaning of faith in the New Testament writings.

One other interesting concept that I found in the *Catholic Encyclopedia* had to do with credibility. When theologians say that a certain statement is incredible, they often mean that it is extraordinary. But the credibility or incredibility of a statement has nothing to do with its probability or improbability; it depends solely on the credentials of the authority that makes the statement.

I found these words consoling and encouraging. In my "Faith 101" course, this statement affirms the value that I place on my experiences of God. When I got into the process of reviewing my journals for this book, I realized that I do not care if a statement about God is incredible or improbable, only that it came from God and not from my imagination. To find out the true source I need discernment. As I said before, the fruits of my "experience of God" will tell me if I can trust it or not. Discernment in its fullness takes a practiced heart, fine-tuned to hear the word of God, and the single-mindedness to follow that word in love. It is truly a gift from God but not one dropped from the skies fully formed. It is a gift cultivated by a prayerful life and the search for self-knowledge.

To discern the Spirit I must live within my life. I must be really present to myself here and now. And at the still-point of my selfhood, in the ambiance of my God-awareness, my God-desire, I choose and respond, continuing to notice the congruence of my choice with my God-desire, and my growing freedom for love as I live out the consequences. Discernment requires bringing my present life situation to where God touches me.[4]

I wonder if I really qualify as a person of faith. I have seen so many natural wonders in my travels, so much beauty; I have experienced the presence of God in my life so often, in good and in bad times. I have felt the love of God carrying me during my illnesses.

I have seen polar bears face to face, eagles soaring above my head, and a moose a few steps away from me. I have spent hours watching a family of bison from the car just a few feet away without any incident. I have traveled to other countries and visited the village in northern Spain where my father was born. I have crossed the Arctic Circle and visited native villages. I have seen orcas and porpoises swimming alongside our tour boat as if they were dancing with us. I have seen creation as God's playground!

I could go on, but the most important part of this story is that for most of my life working for the Church, my salary never reached $20,000 annually. I have done all this traveling using credit cards and saving in other areas. In other words, I am not rich!

I have a wonderful family. All the pain my brother and I went through when our father died and when we came from Cuba made us very close. His wife is my best friend, and I have a great relationship with my two nieces and my nephew. These children are the apples of my eye, and the fact that I wear glasses makes them seem brighter.

I am blessed by my Franciscan community and wonderful friends. Just like my father and my brother, I love photography, and through my magic lens I penetrate the secrets of creation.

I have been blessed with the opportunity to serve with poor, sick, and marginalized people. I am grateful for the many couples and single people who have trusted me to walk with them for parts of their own journeys. My ministry has allowed me to see, and I mean "see" the presence of God in many lives.

I have worked alongside good and not so good people—people who can dream and others who suffer from severe myopic vision, people who respect me and people who cannot suffer my presence. All of them are beloved of God, and when a hurricane strikes in South Florida nobody escapes its force.

Is this faith, I wonder? The little that I have seen "*teaches me to trust the Creator for all I have not seen.*" How could I not have faith?

I am grateful for the opportunities that life has given me to meet wisdom people, women and men who have guided me and shared their vision with me.

I am very grateful that at some point in my life, someone encouraged me to keep journals. My journals are not neat or orderly. Some are notebooks, some entries are on pieces of paper or on old used envelopes; nonetheless, they capture my memories lest I forget my weakest moments or my deepest experiences of God.

I could not write a chapter on faith without going back to some of my notes. They keep safe what my memory has already deleted.

Journal
On Suffering
April 30, 1994
11:30 P.M.

I am in a lot of pain! My right shoulder, arm, neck, and head hurt a lot. Nights are very hard. I felt bad before I left home to come to the office, but now is really, really bad. I am nervous and worried. It is a nagging pain and it scares me. I feel that my physical condition is getting worse.

The arthritis pain is almost unbearable in spite of the new medicine. I am scared, not frozen yet, but at least I feel that I can "embrace" these feelings.

I read an article in an issue of *Human Development* magazine that challenged me to "self-discovery within an illness." The deterioration of my body calls me to new wholeness. My strong, realistic self can help, but the profound questions of life, death, and immortality are not

> touched. Unless we experience a dramatic illness we live in our fantasies about life undisturbed, we spend most of our time avoiding the richer questions of life and death.
>
> This is a moment of transition in my life. I feel that the old me is eroding away and the new person is not yet born. This makes me weak and vulnerable.
>
> Somehow, the Gospel verse, "Jesus, remember me when you come into your kingdom," came to mind. I was singing it in my head and feeling deeply moved, very small, insignificant, and vulnerable. So much so, that I was begging Jesus to "remember me"; I was sure that somehow I had been overlooked. . . . These were strong, unusual feelings. My office became Golgotha and even the crucifix on my wall looked higher and distant. I felt totally abandoned and forgotten.
>
> Tonight I went to Mass, and when a Sister whom I don't know gave me Communion, she said looking into my eyes, "Take courage!" I was deeply touched. Perhaps there is a reason for all this pain.

As I try to remember the details of what happened that day, my memory takes a lunch break. I have to trust my own words in my journal, and what I read gives me chills. Did I realize then the touch of God through the Sister? Did I feel the healing and the reassurance of God's presence in the midst of my pain? Obviously, I do not have the answer, but I am filled with gratitude for the awesome love of God, who found a way to touch me in the middle of so much physical and spiritual pain.

Again, it is a matter of faith. Can I prove that those "little miracles" really happened? I quote from my journals precisely because that makes the experiences real for me, and for you, the reader.

There are only two ways to live . . .
one is as though nothing is a miracle . . .
the other is as if everything is.

—Albert Einstein

Journal
Sin
May 3, 1995
4:30 P.M.

I am at the University of St. Mary of the Lakes in Mundelein, Illinois, where I will be a speaker for the American Correctional Chaplains Association. Well, my talks are prepared and I feel good about them . . .

These past weeks I have been struggling with the fact that I have to accept my physical limitations, and even more, enjoy them! My cross and challenge is to accept myself as a limited creature while at other times I experience oneness with the universe. To be in touch with the infinite and also with my limited reality. Is this incarnation?

There is one word that keeps coming to mind: healing. Only God can heal me from the immaturity (sin?) of wanting to be "god-like" right now. Perhaps I should leave this in God's hands, but that is very difficult for me to do. In a way this sounds like the original sin of St. Augustine: to be god without God.

I think I am fighting God . . .

If I say I need God, I'll be acknowledging my limitations and I don't want to do that. Therefore, I have to become "super-woman" to be able to make it by myself. It is true that I am very smart, but there are others smarter than me. I refuse to accept that possibility and shelter myself in an individualism that is really nothing but a defense. I don't want anyone to make me face the fact that I am as limited as the rest, in spite of the fact that I might have a superior intelligence.

10:30 P.M.

Have mercy on me, O God,
and cleanse me from my sin . . .
Create in me a clean heart, O God,
and put a new spirit within me . . .

—Psalm 51

To be healed I have to become vulnerable and open up, that means nakedness in front of you, myself, and others. I am afraid of being vulnerable; it's so easy to get hurt. My God, how easily people hurt me!

It is difficult to relate to Jesus; he shows me a different you: a suffering, broken God. Is that who you are? Do you feel pain? Do you cry? Did you get hurt by my stupid words early today? Does this mean that you are not anymore the "uncaused cause," the "unmoved mover," the impassible God out there in heaven?

You ask me to move on again; to leave my "land" trusting only in your promise. I don't know if I can do it!

Again, this is all about faith. Who do I think I am? Am I going back to my teenage years and my stupid doubts? I am surprised by my journal entries. I know I wrote them, because at the time I did not have a computer, and it is my handwriting; I also found the little symbols that I liked to draw here and there.

For a long time, since I was made aware of its presence, I have drawn support and strength from the "cloud of witnesses" that surrounds us. These people lived and died strengthened by their faith, and today we stand on their shoulders.

> *Faith is the assurance of things hoped for, the conviction of things not seen. . . . By faith we understand that the worlds were prepared by the word of God, so that what is seen was made from things that are not visible. Therefore, since we are surrounded by so great a cloud of witnesses, let us also lay aside every weight and the sin that clings so closely, and let us run with perseverance the race that is set before us, looking to Jesus the pioneer and perfecter of our faith.*
>
> —Hebrews 11:1-3; 12:1-2

Fear Ends Where Faith Begins

Reading my journals helped me to follow my own growth and to identify spiritual processes, which I believe can benefit everyone. One of them is the change and development of my images of God. My first image was the compassionate and loving God who welcomed my father into heaven. From there I moved to Jesus, who put a human face to my "heavenly" God, and I also began to become familiar with the Gospel message.

It was Jesus who told the parable of the Prodigal Son, so similar to my experience with my father, and I fell in love with Jesus. He and his message guided my life for years and gave me the values that I still live by today. In the Gospel I found the truth and the truth set me free (John 8:32). Two things happened at this point: First, I was focusing my prayer and readings on the historical Jesus and the events of his human life. Second, my ministry required the preparation of a lot of liturgical celebrations that emphasized the soteriological understanding of Jesus. I mentioned this earlier when I wrote about God, but the fact is that the questioning did not begin overnight, it was a long process.

One very good example is one of the lines that we find in the Easter Proclamation: "O happy fault, O necessary sin of Adam that gained for us so great a Redeemer!" A few times I even had to sing it in church, although I did not believe what it implied. The words suggest that the sin of Adam was necessary for Christ to come. By then, I was uncomfortable with that concept and believed as I do today that Christ would have come with or without Adam's sin.

I was beginning to touch and be touched by the Creator God of the universe, while the historical Jesus was becoming less important in my prayer and in my daily life. I was "living" Jesus' words recorded in the Gospel according to John:

> *Father, the hour has come; glorify your Son so that the Son may glorify you. . . . I glorified you on earth by finishing the work that you gave me to do. So now, Father, glorify me in your own presence with the glory that I had in your presence before the world existed.*
>
> —John 17:1-5

Now that the human Jesus had "finished the work that the Father had given him to do," I felt that the risen, Cosmic Christ was doing something new that I could not express in the traditional liturgical prayers. The appeal was that he took me beyond the historical Jesus, the institutional church, Western civilization, Christendom, and even the planet. I was getting to experience and feel the presence of the universal Christ, the Christ that did not belong only to Christians or to specific churches.

This Christ was very attractive, but it posed a danger: he could be so awesome and "cosmic" that a personal relationship with him was difficult. Was it possible to enter into a loving relationship with the Omega Point? It was then that I turned even more to the concept of mystery, a companion that became indispensable in my journey of faith. I could not understand what I was feeling, but I knew that I was on the right track. I believed in the Christ, but I also believed that in his humanity Jesus had revealed the face of God. These two points did not contradict each other.

I stopped trying to "teach" about God and started to listen more to the spiritual experiences of the various people that I was meeting for spiritual guidance. I held on to my belief that God is not an abstract, otherworldly deity removed from this world to dwell in statues, cathedrals, or theological systems. God is very busy with the care of the world. And one department that takes a great amount of time is the suffering-humanity department. In that department God has rolled up God's sleeves, plunged in with both feet, turned God's face to the sick and sorrowing, and set to work liberating the captives. That is the meaning of the cross, and that is God's comforting word over the problem of evil.[5] I held on to that God, the God of my faith, the God of Jesus, and also of Mystery.

In my travels I came to know the many faces of God, all true, all different, and all impossible to explain or analyze. God became amazing, and this gave me security and strength to face anything that life gave me. The only setback was that I did not have the appropriate words to describe this new relationship with the personal and transcendent God.

I am sure that many readers will relate to my predicament. The God I believe in is the Creator, the Omega Point, the beginning and the end, and at the same time my friend, my companion on the journey, and the One in whom I live, move, and have my being. These facets of the One God seemed irreconcilable.

In my journals, I also discovered that the easiest way for the devil to get to us is fear. This was very obvious in my writings, and it deserves a place in this book.

Fear

Fear is that which stands between me and the freedom that God created me for. It is a powerful emotion, ranging from anxiety to terror that generally paralyzes one. It is experienced when we encounter someone or something that threatens our life, our security, or our well-being. For some, God has been a source of fear, the One who has the power to send us to hell for not being Christians, as in the case of my father.

For others it is the devil, the one who can make us do what we do not want to do, one who is full of lies and capable of seduction. "There is no fear in love, but perfect love casts out fear. For fear has to do with punishment, and he who fears is not perfected in love" (1 John 4:18).

Some of the negative consequences of fear are paralysis, hysterical activity, loss of courage, panic attacks, timidity, and hesitation. I am not referring to the "fear of God," the awe that we feel when we witness divine activity in the world. By fear I mean that negative, hopeless feeling we experience when facing an impending disaster or a painful situation that we do not feel capable of overcoming. This fear paralyzes and diminishes the person. It reduces the person to a puppet under its control. The New Testament is filled of admonitions to the disciples, "Do not fear! Fear is useless."

> *Then there appeared to him an angel of the Lord. . . . When Zechariah saw him, he was terrified; and fear overwhelmed him. But the angel said to him, "Do not be afraid, Zechariah."*
>
> —Luke 1:11-13

When we allow fear to overwhelm us, it can lead to a withdrawal from God, as in the garden. The relationship based on trust is destroyed, and fear takes its place.

According to the Genesis story, Adam did not trust God to provide him with "divinity." He was destined to be fully "divinized" by God in glory, but, seduced by the devil, he wanted to "be like God" but "without God, before God, and not in accordance with God."[6] How many times I have tried the same and do things "my way!"

> *The Lord God then called to the man and asked him, "Where are you?" He answered, "I heard you in the garden; but I was afraid, because I was naked, so I hid myself."*
>
> —Genesis 3:9-10

Whether one takes the story at face value or as part of a mythological account of creation, the truth of the message is the same: if we sever our relationship with God and decide to do things our way, we will end up being afraid because the "ground of our being" has been rejected.

In the story, the man and the woman are the ones in hiding; they want to avoid God's seeing them and talking with them. When God asks Adam *where he is*, he is not talking about a place. God can see everything; God is really asking, "What has happened to you? What is this unnatural condition of being afraid of me?" Adam is closing his ears to the voice of the One who made him, the One who knows him thoroughly, the One whose breath brought movement to Adam's limbs. Adam hides from the One who gave him life. Few scenes portray so vividly the sadness and twisted vision of that reality which is human alienation.[7]

Adam is afraid of God! Some terrible disorder has inserted itself into creation if men and women feel they have to escape the gaze of the Lord. Being uncovered and totally open to God's view is the state God intended for humans. What reason is there to hide from God?[8]

The human Jesus trusted God, as did Mary and many others throughout our history. "Do not fear, only believe" (Mark 5:36). The causes of our fears may not be that "biblical" or even religious. Often we do not even think that they are interfering with our relationship with God.

Recently, a friend told me the story of something that had happened to her when she was a child.

> I was four years old when I decided to ride a big bicycle by myself. I ended up losing control and crashing into a fence surrounded by bushes with thorns. I bled and hurt and my mother, almost hysterical,

> told me that it had been a very stupid thing to do and that I should have known better.
>
> She also emphasized that I should learn the lesson from the bike: "Never try something that you cannot control, handle, or understand. I was horrified of bicycles until I was a teenager," she continued, "actually, was I afraid of bicycles, or of failing and looking stupid?"
>
> I have become an adult who is very careful to try new things and who avoids the unknown as well as challenging situations and individuals. All this because of a bike!

After finishing the story, she said, "Fear tells me to stop what I am doing and I remain 'stuck' in my 'safe' place where no bicycle or bush with thorns can hurt me."

My friend is having a hard time trusting in God's Providence and love. Behind every experience of God, there is always the ghost of fear lurking in the background. She will need to be healed from it before she can really accept the love of God, which is freely given even if she cannot ride a bike.

I wonder if fear was born when we began hiding from God and continues today when we hide not only from God but also from others and even from ourselves. There is an anonymous saying that I love:

> If I can endure for this minute whatever is happening to me no matter how heavy my heart is or how dark the moment might be. . . . If I can but keep on believing what I know in my heart to be true, that darkness will fade with morning and that this will pass away, too. . . . Then nothing can ever disturb me

> or fill me with uncertain fear, for as sure as night brings dawning, my morning is bound to appear.

I wish I had written this beautiful and poetic piece; it describes my attitude towards life, faith, and hope.

Yes, life is hard, but God is soooo good!

There is a New Testament story that captures the way I try to handle my fears and any other unknown that life might present. It is taken from the Gospel of Matthew 14:22-31 (paraphrased):

> One day, Jesus asked the disciples to take the boat and go to the other side, while he dismissed the crowds. Afterwards he went up the mountain by himself to pray. When evening came, he was there alone.
>
> The boat was far from land fighting a strong wind.
>
> Early in the morning he came walking toward them on the lake, but the disciples were terrified, saying, "It is a ghost!" And they cried out in fear. Jesus spoke to them and said, "Take heart, it is I; do not be afraid."
>
> In his usual emotive way Peter said, "Lord, if it is you, command me to come to you on the water." He said, "Come." So Peter got out of the boat, started walking on the water, and came toward Jesus. Peter had heard the words of his Master and in trust began to walk on water.
>
> I think he would have made it all the way, except for the fact that, at some point, he took his eyes off

> Jesus and started paying attention to the strong wind.
>
> Immediately, he became frightened, and began to sink. When he cried out, "Lord, save me!" Jesus reached out his hand and caught him, saying, "You of little faith, why did you doubt?"

I have experienced that fear as I am sure many others have. As long as I keep my eyes on God, God's love and goodness, I have nothing to fear. When I instead focus on the storms, the pain, the problems, or even on the fact that I am "walking on water," I sink!

> Fear knocked at the door. Faith answered.
> And lo, no one was there.
>
> —Old English Proverb

Journal
August 26, 2001
4:00 P.M.

We just returned from two weeks of vacation in the mountains of Northwestern Canada. It is good, from time to time, being able to spend a few days to enjoy the beauty of the world God has created. Even with a temperature of eighty-five degrees, we could see the snow on top of the mountains. The contrast of the sun, blue sky, turquoise lakes and snow was incredible.

We took a cable car to the top of a mountain and saw how the landscape was changing, evergreens reaching out under the strong sunlight and the snow.

The smell of the pines made me dizzy. Living in South Florida, I forget how overwhelming the smell of new pines is. When I thought that it was not possible to experience more beauty, I saw a mama bear with her cub, very well-behaved following her footprints. We saw several moose, strong and imposing with their gigantic antlers. A majestic eagle was busy building a nest on top of a pine.

Coming down the mountains, we rested by a lake; I found myself walking next to some sheep that did not seem to be bothered by my presence. The sheep were losing wool to protect themselves from the strong heat, which is uncommon in this area. They did not need a barber or a shepherd to fleece them. God had already provided for these needs when they were created.

I felt as if the whole creation were singing a canticle of praise to the Creator:

Praise the LORD!
Praise the LORD from the heavens;
Praise him in the heights!
. . . .
Praise him, sun and moon;
praise him, all you shining stars!
Praise him, you highest heavens,
and you waters above the heavens!
Let them praise the name of the LORD,
for he commanded and they were created.
He established them forever and ever.
. . . .
Praise the LORD from the earth,
you sea monsters and all deeps,
fire and hail, snow and frost,
stormy wind fulfilling his command!
Mountains and all hills,
fruit trees and all cedars!
Wild animals and all cattle,
creeping things and flying birds!
. . . .
Praise the Lord!

—Psalm 148:1-10, 14

Perhaps because I lead Bible classes, I thought about a question I often hear: When will the world end? Today some people think that God will destroy the world soon and establish his kingdom on earth. In the midst of the beauty and the natural order that I was experiencing, I could only say, "My God, how great you are!"

I do not think that the destruction of God's creation is consistent with the understanding of the Christian message. "In him [Christ] all things in heaven and on earth were created . . . all things have been created through him and for him. He himself is before all things, and in him all things hold together" (Colossians 1:16-17).

If Christ is the beginning and the end, then this creation is Christ-centered, and destruction does not seem to be a part of God's plan. However, in our abused freedom, we are capable of self-destruction. I wonder how come I do not hear that concern more frequently in Christian circles.

I think it is easier to speculate about what God will or will not do with the world than to look at what we are already doing to it. We throw away all types of waste as we hike in the mountains, drop garbage in rivers, lakes and seas and pollute the air.

In the United States, we throw away food if it is not cooked the way we like it, without worrying that so many people in the world are dying from starvation. We waste water, without considering that one-third of the world's population lacks access to safe drinking water.

Why are we so concerned about "the end of the world," or the famous Armageddon, and do not realize that the worst destruction is the one we are causing ourselves?

These thoughts were taking away some of the joy from my trip. With a slightly heavy heart, I arrived at the Sunday Eucharist in the small-town church. Upon entering, I felt at home, even in a foreign country.

In the pew in front of us sat a young couple with six children under the age of ten, including nine-month-old twins. During the Mass, the two babies were passed from arm to arm between the mother, the father, and the brothers. It was difficult to keep six children relatively quiet in a small church. Next to us was an older woman who played with one of them, and to our right, a young man who made them smile all the time.

When the time came for the first reading, a deformed young man went to the podium. He was an exact replica of the famous Quasimodo, the Hunchback of Notre Dame, who with a big smile and poise proclaimed to us the Word of God. In the homily, the priest told us that he and four young people were going on pilgrimage to Toronto representing their diocese at a youth day with the pope. The young man was one of the representatives.

It was then that I realized that God continues recreating every moment, and that in every situation God gives us his love, and that his wishes for us are for life and not death.

I asked for forgiveness for the times that I let the darkness overcome me and did not allow the light to shine.

When we left the church, I realized that the whole creation sang praises to the Creator and that the universe is God's cathedral. The mountains were in the same place, the rivers were still flowing freely, and the four young people were planning their pilgrimage to Toronto.

I felt my hope come alive again, and at that moment I knew that in the midst of the hunchbacks, of those who look healthy, of the mountains and the animals, "The light shines in the darkness, and the darkness did not overcome it" (John 1:5).

Reading this journal entry has stirred up many deep feelings. I am aware that I continue to make the same mistakes. Even now, when I see a person so badly deformed,

I pity him or her. I still think that I "have something on them." How foolish of me. The only difference between us is that their handicaps are obvious and overt, while mine are concealed and covered up. I hope God continues to be patient and merciful with me until one day, perhaps, I grow up.

> *For I am convinced that neither death, nor life, nor angels, nor rulers, nor things present, nor things to come, nor powers, nor height, nor depth, nor anything else in all creation, will be able to separate us from the love of God in Christ Jesus our Lord.*
>
> —Romans 8:38-39

Can I prove all this?

Can I assure others that nothing can separate us from the love of God in Christ Jesus our Lord?

Can I ask my family and friends not to fear the devil because the Light has overcome the darkness?

Can I promise that our sufferings can energize and contribute to the transformation of the Body of Christ and of the universe?

Of course not!

The answer is always faith.

But I can say this: I do not believe in the goodness of God; I do not believe that the light always overcomes the darkness; I do not believe that creation has a purpose or that God is very, very good. I do not believe any of these things that I have written, because *I KNOW* them to be true!

Epilogue

Journal
Today
Now

I just finished the book.

I wanted to present the best theodicy possible, so I shared mine. It is certainly not the best, but it is the best one I have.

The question of the presence of suffering in a world created by a good God is as old as humanity. I knew that I probably did not have the most sophisticated answer, but I was willing to share my own journey, and the answer is found in my own struggle.

Today and now I am comfortable with my writing.

From the moment I started writing, I knew I had to use some of my journals. This book was meant to reflect my experience of God, evil, and suffering, and I could not do that without revisiting my own journey of faith.

What a task! I had to dig in drawers, boxes, filing cabinets, and the like, to find notebooks, loose pages, stapled notes, and yellow pads that supposedly contained the wisdom of my life's journey.

Even if the book was never to be read, I already got more than I bargained for by writing it.

These months of reading and writing have helped me understand and integrate my faith even more.

I can paraphrase a few words from the Gospel of John to describe what I think has happened to me (cf. John 13:2-4):

And a few months ago Adele, knowing that she had come from God and was going to God, sat at her computer, got her journals and began to write this book.

This has been the unexpected gift for the work I have done. I am now surer than ever that I have come from God and am going to God.

Life is hard but God is good. I believe this with all my being. When something unexpected happens to me, I say, "Life gave me this or that." If I thank God for the good things that happen, whom do I blame for the bad ones? So I made the decision to never say, "God has blessed me with good health," but, "I am blessed to have a good health," or "life has been good to me."

I know that "IT" happens and that life is hard, but I am convinced by my own experiences that God is in the mess all the way up to his ears (so to speak).

I will continue to wrestle with the question of a personal relationship with God if God is not a "person." How can I talk with the Ground of my being, the Omega Point, or the Cosmic Christ?

Mystery again! But I am not complaining. I may not be "talking" but we are communicating and in communion, and I think this book reflects that.

Maybe I cannot rest in the "arms" of Jesus, but I can let myself "fall" into the One in whom I breathe, and move, and have my being.

I am not interested in having holy cards with the "image" of Jesus or in venerating the Shroud of Turin. It does not really matter what Jesus looked like historically, because now his physical body has been transformed.

I like to rest in the One who "is before all things, and in whom all things hold together" (see Colossians 1:15-17).

In less than two months I will have a total knee replacement. I am a bit concerned because it is my right knee and I need it to drive. Driving is important to me, and I will have to depend on family and friends for the first few months.

Also, other physical issues can cause setbacks with the surgery and my doctors are trying to cover all the bases.

They tell me that the rehabilitation process will be very painful so I hope that I can continue to embrace pain so it does not turn into suffering for me and others.

I also hope that if I join my pain/suffering to that of all the sick people of the world, the energy that we can create will move us forward in the universal process of transformation.

I also worry about our world, our country, and everyone and everything in it. But I choose to trust.

Just as many years ago I decided to live as if I had faith, today I choose to continue to live as if I had hope.

I believe that in the midst of the hardness of life, there is a God who is very good and who is available to everyone.

God's desire for us is stronger than our desire for God; that is why God will never give up on us.

I now move on to other endeavors.

I can't wait to see the children whom I have missed terribly during this time of writing.

I am not writing from a little cabin overlooking the river or the mountains. I am home in the middle of everything, in the middle of "IT" and surrounded by love and friendship. Brother pain will continue to walk with me as my faithful companion.

But, as I have said before, all will be well. In whatever manner it will be well.

I don't believe it. I KNOW it!

Notes

1. The Journey to Understanding Begins

1. G. K. Chesterton, *What's Wrong with the World* (New York: Dodd, Mead, 1910), chap. 5.

2. Seeking and Finding God

1. *Catechism of the Catholic Church* (United States Catholic Conference, 1994; New York: Doubleday, 1995) §206.
2. Pierre Teilhard de Chardin, *The Divine Milieu* (1960; repr., New York: Perennial Classics, 2001), 101.
3. Richard Heffern, "The Eternal Christ in the Cosmic Story," interview with Richard Rohr, *National Catholic Reporter*, December 11, 2009 (http://ncronline.org).
4. Catherine Mowry LaCugna, *God for Us: The Trinity and Christian Life* (New York: HarperCollins, 1991).
5. See *Catechism of the Catholic Church*, §§218-21, 232-45, 261-67.
6. Ibid., §§236-37.
7. Pierre Teilhard de Chardin, *The Phenomenon of Man* (New York: Harper & Row, 1959), 250-75.

8. Steven R. Watkins, *Flannery O'Connor and Teilhard de Chardin* (New York: Peter Lang, 2009), 74.

9. John W. de Gruchy, ed., *Letters and Papers from Prison* (Dietrich Bonhoeffer Works 8; Minneapolis: Fortress Press, 2009), 534.

10. First Council of Ephesus (431) and Council of Chalcedon (451).

11. http://www.wired.com/threatlevel/2007/09/nebraska-senato/#ixzz0wD8Nna2X.

12. Robert L. Faricy, "Teilhard de Chardin on Creation and the Christian Life," *Theology Today* 23, no. 4 (1967): 512.

13. Pierre Teilhard de Chardin, *The Divine Milieu: An Essay on the Interior Life* (New York: Harper & Row, 1968), 112.

3. The Mystery of Evil

1. Hans Küng, *Christianity and Chinese Religions* (New York: Doubleday, 1989), 174.

2. United States Conference of Catholic Bishops, The New American Bible online, Hosea, Introduction, http://www.usccb.org/nab/bible/hosea/intro.htm.

3. Ibid.

4. Anne Frank, quotation from BrainyQuote.com (Xplore Inc, 2010) http://www.brainyquote.com/quotes/authors/a/anne_frank.html (accessed July 29, 2010).

5. Henri Rondet, *Original Sin: The Patristic and Theological Background* (Staten Island, NY: Alba House, 1972), 39.

6. Anthony T. Padovano, *Original Sin and Christian Anthropology* (Washington, DC: Corpus Books, 1969), 21.

7. Rondet, *Original Sin,* 37-38.

8. Ibid., 39.

9. Peter Kreeft, "The Problem of Evil," chap. 7 in Peter Kreeft, *Fundamentals of the Faith: Essays in Christian Apologetics* (San Francisco: Ignatius Press, 1988), 54-58.

10. Ilia Delio, *Christ in Evolution* (Maryknoll, NY: Orbis Books, 2008), 8.

11. St. Thomas Aquinas, *Summa Theologica*, I, q.48, a.1.

12. Stephen J. Duffy, "Evil," in *The New Dictionary of Catholic Spirituality*, ed. Michael Downey (Collegeville, MN: Liturgical Press, 1993), 362.

13. *Catechism of the Catholic Church*, §§391, 394.

14. Ibid., §2851.

15. Ibid., §414

16. *New American Bible* (Washington, DC: Confraternity of Christian Doctrine, Inc., 1991), note 18.

17. *Catechism of the Catholic Church*, §395.

18. Kreeft, "Problem of Evil," 54-58.

19. *Catechism of the Catholic Church*, §§1033, 1035.

20. Pope John Paul II, Apostolic Exhortation, *Reconciliation and Penance*, December 2, 1984, 16.

21. See http://www.americancatholic.org/news/JustWar/iraq/papalstatement.asp (emphasis added). See Catholic News Service, January 7, 2008.

22. Rich Heffern, "The Eternal Christ in the Cosmic Story," interview with Richard Rohr, *National Catholic Reporter*, December 11, 2009, http://ncronline.org.

23. Pierre Teilhard de Chardin, "La vie cosmique" (1916), in *Écrits du temps de la guerre: 1916-1919* (Paris: Seuil, 1965), 48.

24. Pierre Teilhard de Chardin, "The Evolution of Chastity" (Peking, February 1934), in *Toward the Future* (London: Collins, 1975), 86-87.

4. Understanding Anger and Forgiveness

1. Quoted on the Web page of the Roman Catholic Diocese of Pembroke, Ontario, and Quebec, Canada, http://diocesepembroke.ca/site/index.php.

2. Some notes taken from my book *Anger: A Positive Energy* (Hollywood, FL: Get-With-It, 2004). Used with the author's permission.

3. *Catechism of the Catholic Church*, §§1767, 1768, 1774.

5. The Mystery of Suffering

1. Albert Nolan, O.P., *Hope in an Age of Despair: And Other Talks and Writings* (Maryknoll, NY: Orbis Books, 2009), 9-10.

2. Richard Sparks, C.S.P., "Suffering," in *The New Dictionary of Catholic Spirituality*, ed. Michael Downey (Collegeville, MN: Liturgical Press, 1993), 951.

3. Thomas Merton, *The Seven Storey Mountain* (New York: Houghton Mifflin Harcourt, 1999), 91.

4. Columna Cary-Elwes, *Experiences with God: A Dictionary of Spirituality* (London: Sheed & Ward, 1986), 49.

5. St. Francis of Assisi, "Testament," in *Omnibus of Sources*, ed. Marion A. Habig (Chicago: Franciscan Herald Press, 1973), 67.

6. St. Francis of Assisi, "Rule of 1223," in *Omnibus of Sources*, 61.

7. Sister Frances Teresa Downing, OSC, *Living the Incarnation: Praying with Francis and Clare of Assisi* (London: Darton, Longman & Todd, 1993), 69.

8. Albert Nolan, *Jesus Today: A Spirituality of Radical Freedom* (Maryknoll, NY: Orbis Books, 2007), 180.

9. Robert Ellsberg, *The Saints' Guide to Happiness* (New York: North Point Press, 2003), xi.

10. Arthur Livingston, *The Little Flowers of St. Francis of Assisi* (New York: Heritage Press, 1965), chap. 8.

11. William J. O'Malley, *Redemptive Suffering: Understanding Suffering, Living with It, Growing through It* (New York: Crossroad, 1997), 103.

12. Richard Rohr, *The Naked Now: Learning to See as the Mystics See* (New York: Crossroad, 2009), 124-25.

13. Reinhold Niebuhr, *The Essential Reinhold Niebuhr: Selected Essays and Addresses,* ed. Robert McAfee Brown (New Haven, CT: Yale University Press, 1987), 251.

14. Pierre Teilhard de Chardin, "Redemptive Suffering," in Pierre Teilhard de Chardin, *Hymn of the Universe* (1965; repr., London: Fountain Books, 1977), 85-86.

15. Rohr, *Naked Now*, 129-30.

16. Vatican II, *Gaudium et Spes* (Pastoral Constitution on the Church in the Modern World), December 7, 1965, art. 18.

6. Understanding Faith

1. Dorothy Herrmann, *Helen Keller: A Life* (Chicago: University of Chicago Press, 1999), 297.

2. *The Collected Works of Ralph Waldo Emerson* (London: Routledge, 1897), 502.

3. "Faith," in *The Catholic Encyclopedia* (New York: Robert Appleton, 1907-12), http://www.newadvent.org/cathen/05752c.htm (accessed August 30, 2010).

4. Ernest E. Larkin, O. Carm. *Silent Presence* (Rockaway, NJ: Dimension Books, 1998).

5. Jerry Robbins, "The Mystery of Evil," *Word & World* 19 (1999): 381-88.

6. *Catechism of the Catholic Church*, §398.

7. William Reiser, S.J., "Adam in Hiding," *Spirituality Today* 38 (1986): 242-53.

8. Ibid.